MW00619073

otl aicher

the world as
design

with an introduction
by wolfgang jean stock

Ernst & Sohn
A Wiley Brand

published in co-operation with the
otl aicher archives

library of congress card no.:
applied for

british library cataloguing-in-publication data
a catalogue record for this book is available from the british library.

bibliographic information published by
the deutsche nationalbibliothek
the deutsche nationalbibliothek lists this publication in the
deutsche nationalbibliografie; detailed bibliographic data are
available on the internet at <http://dnb.d-nb.de>.

translation: michael robinson
translation of the amended preface: übersetzungen hanns schie-
fele, bad reichenhall, germany

typesetting: thomson digital, noida, india

2. edition

print isbn: 978-3-433-03117-9
epdf isbn: 978-3-433-60584-4
epub isbn: 978-3-433-60583-7
emobi isbn: 978-3-433-60582-0
obook isbn: 978-3-433-60585-1

contents

Otl Aicher was a good friend, mentor and working colleague. There was never a division between conversations on our work or any other subject – the topics ranged far and wide. Often as he was talking, Otl would pick up a piece of paper and illustrate his point with careful strokes of a ball-point. The combination was uniquely personal – witty, incisive and often thought-provoking.

During his summer retreats in August at Rotis, Otl would commit his thoughts to paper and these later became the subject of two books. Before then some of them had appeared randomly as articles in magazines or in editions. I remember being frustrated because I could not read German, even though I might guess at their content from the many hours spent with Otl hearing their story lines. I was also upset because I so much wanted to share Otl's insights with others around me; he seemed to be able to say with clarity and eloquence many of the things I felt needed to be said – as well as some of the things which we did not agree about. In his last years Otl was, I felt, at the height of his creativity in many fields, which ranged from visual communication and new typefaces to political and philosophical comment.

Following the tragedy of Otl's death I felt compelled to help make it possible for all of his writings to be translated and published in English. Otl saw through the stupidities of fashion and vanity. His opinions were so relevant to the issues of today that I believed it was important for them to be shared with a wider English-speaking audience – relevant to my own generation as well as students, professionals and the lay public.

Otl wrote rather in the way that he spoke and after some debate with those who were closer to him and who were also German speakers it was decided to leave the translation in its conversational form. We also felt that it was important to respect Otl's passionate objection to capital letters for starting sentences of marking traditionally important words. Perhaps it underlined his scorn for the pompous.

There was an integrity about the way that Otl lived, practised and preached. He would probably have been uncomfortable with the word preach, but I use it here in its most honourable and inspiring sense.

Norman Foster
London, January 1994

Introduction

by Wolfgang Jean Stock

1

In 1950, on a very early visit to the Federal Republic, Hannah Arendt noted: "If you watch the Germans bustling and stumbling through the ruins of their thousand-year-old history, you realize that this bustling has become their principal weapon for protecting themselves against reality."

Two years after currency reform and five years after the end of the war the shock of defeat and horror about the crimes committed in the name of Germany had been largely suppressed. In the face of everyday privations the majority of West Germans had accustomed themselves to the normality of survival. Responsibility for the causes and consequences of the Nazi regime was left aside amidst the compulsory reality of occupation and handling shortages. People began vigorous clearance of the fields of rubble, but the rubble inside them stayed where it was. Finally the Nuremberg trials worked as a kind of general absolution from the outside.

"Rebuilding" became the slogan and stimulus of the times. As early as 1948, in the *Frankfurter Hefte*, Walter Dirks pointed out how treacherous this word, increasingly interpreted as restoring the old order, could be. Anyone who spoke up for a new social and cultural structure rather than rebuilding the old state of things was unwittingly placed on the fringes of Wirtschaftswunder society, which was forming early. No wonder that a large number of cultural initiatives, particularly non-conformist newspapers and publishing houses, had to give up.

2

But one small group preparing around 1950 to find a new kind of higher educational establishment in Ulm on the Danube, managed to make a success of it. Inge Scholl and Otl Aicher had found out how great was the need for a new cultural direction in their work at the Volkshochschule in Ulm. With their friends they drew up a programme for a school of design on socio-political lines. Their educational concept combined an anti-fascist attitude with democratic hope. Graphics were to become social communication, and product design was to encourage humanization of everyday life. After a number of difficulties, especially in terms of finance, teaching started at the Hochschule für Gestaltung (HfG) in summer 1953. Two years later it moved into its own building, designed by Max Bill, on the Kuhberg in Ulm. The HfG wanted to work as a successor of the Bauhaus from its heights above the Danube valley, admittedly with a fundamental difference. While the Bauhaus saw training in fine art as a requirement for the design of good industrial form, the HfG stood for a direct, functional approach to the matter in hand. For this reason Ulm had no studios for painters and sculptors and no craft workshops.

In his essay "bauhaus and ulm", which is the biographical key to the essays and lectures collected here, Otl Aicher emphasizes this distinction: "at that time in ulm we had to get back to matters, to things, to products, to the street, to the everyday, to people. we had to turn round. it was not about extending art into the everyday world, for example, into application. it was about counter-art, the work of civilization, the culture of civilization."

This also shows the strong feelings of the man coming back from the war, born in 1922, for whom "coming to terms with reality" was on the agenda, and not a concern with pure aesthetics. Thus HfG was dominated by the view that art was an expression of escape from life. But above all the intention was to keep the field of product design free of artistic demands, to avoid formalism.

3

Once more the German provinces became the home of modernity and progress. As was the case with the Bauhaus in Weimar and Dessau, a middle-sized town did not merely offer the possibility of concentrated work. The restricted nature of the milieu, along with local reservations and animosity, were particular factors in compelling HfG to explain and justify its practice. In this tension they felt independent on the Kuhberg – and they really were independent. The Geschwister-Scholl Foundation as an independent source of finance guaranteed a relatively large distance from the state, and the school's own income, often half its annual budget, reinforced selfconfidence.

As an institution, HfG was a dwarf, but its influence was felt world-wide. What drew students from 49 nations to Ulm? Certainly the advanced syllabus, with the social dimensions of design at its centre, and also its educational aims, including training in argument and education that went beyond the subject rather than being specific to it. Admittedly it was essential for the success of HfG that the pioneering spirit of the founders rubbed off on teachers and students. There was a hint of the Messianic in the commitment to building up a new industrial culture: from product design and individual communication via information systems to serial building. Technology and science were to put into effect this forward-looking design of everyday culture.

In the conservative cultural climate of post-war West German society, HfG was a creative island. It held its own until 1968 as an experimental institution at a time when elections were won with the slogan "no experiments". It taught social and cultural responsibility with a view to the future precisely at the time when the universities were reactivating the bourgeois, museum-style canon of education. Faced with the "thousand-year fug" and the plushy cosiness of the economically successful republic, Ulm was looking for practical ways towards enlightenment, criticism and authenticity. In this way the outlines of a functional, democratic culture of things, open to the world, grew up in the midst of West German "neo-Biedermeier".

HfG itself and also the devices, corporate images, printed items and building systems developed there were perceived as evidence of a "different Germany" in countries abroad that were as suspicious as they always had been. The lack of frills, indeed the austerity of the objects and designs showed a farewell to the "clear being". Like the German pavilion by Egon Eiermann and Sep Ruf for the 1958 World Fair in Brussels, the Ulm creations were convincing because of the unity of technology, functionality and aesthetics.

If there was one person who could fundamentally make his mark on the development of HfG as a teacher and model it was Otl Aicher. He represented personal continuity from the preparatory phase onwards, but also got his way in the two great clashes: the question of whether art should be part of the syllabus, which was decided against, leading to the departure of Max Bill in 1957, and in the early sixties in the dispute between "theoreticians" and "practitioners". Aicher took the priority of practical work for granted. In 1963 he inveighed sharply against "uncritical faith in academic theory with its inflated tendency to analysis and increasing impotence in terms of doing".

4

No master without an apprenticeship: HfG was an outstanding school for its teachers as well, perhaps for them in particular. Otl Aicher explained and sharpened up his view of a realism that was not untypical of the early sixties in conflicts between theory and practice that were built into the programme. Martin Walser wrote at the time, for example: "As this realism is not an arbitrary invention, but simply a long overdue way of looking at and presenting things, one can say that it will make possible a further step towards overcoming ideabased, idealistic, ideological approaches." What Walser hoped for literature became Aicher's maxim for the correct use of things.

Aicher always retained his optimism about affecting the shape of the world, which was a motive force behind the whole of HfG. But his opposition to a belief in an ability to plan circumstances also goes back to his Ulm experiences. Today Aicher is clear that large-scale social and economic planning using technical processes and scientific perceptions as instruments, is an invalid means of humanizing the world. However efficient individual areas may be, they actually accelerate the breakdown of social ties and devastation of the planet to the point of endangering the fundamentals of human existence. As man has increasingly made the world into an artefact his inability to control development has grown. Because the production of things follows abstract rules, they subjugate the living world.

For this reason Aicher campaigns for a radical return to consideration of the individual. Instead of trusting governments, economic powers or spiritual courts of appeal, people should develop a need "to live according to their own ideas, to carry out work determined by their own notions, to proceed according to their own concepts". Only then will they not be controlled by circumstances, but shape their own lives. Activity based on such reflections designs things on the criterion of their use and not in expectation of abstract exchange values. The correctness of the design emerges from whether the result is appropriate to the task examined from all sides. The question why is replaced by the question for what purpose. Purpose has to be tested for meaning.

This concrete utopia lies behind more than forty years of Aicher's activity as a designer of posters, sign systems, books, exhibitions, corporate images and his own typeface. In his confrontation with work from industry, services businesses and the media he has developed a design principle that is fundamentally different from design in the popular sense. For him design is precisely not surface design or the production of visual stimuli. This means that Post-Modernism with its borrowings from art and fashion is a regression into randomness and waste. Its formalism follows the cult of the superfluous and it is not for nothing that is reaches its peak in the "useful object that can no longer be used". A need to assert validity has supressed use: styling instead of design.

5

Design means relating thinking and doing. Aesthetics without ethics tend towards deception. It is about the product as a whole, not just about its outward form. The criterion of use also includes social and ecological effects: "design relates to the cultural condition of an epoch, of the period, of the world. the modern world is defined by its design condition. modern civilization is one that is made by man, and therefore designed. the quality of the designs is the quality of the world."

Design of this kind requires appropriate partners. In his insider's view of doing things, Aicher also cites institutional reasons for why not every person giving a commission is suitable. Firstly original design requires complete commitment from all involved. It then needs the culture of the "round-table" at which businessmen, engineers and designers consult each other. Because small and medium-sized businesses are manageable and their structures less alienated, they are most suited for the emergence of original design. Aicher: "design is the life process of a business, when intentions should concretize into facts and phenomena. it is the centre of business culture, of innovative and creative concern with the purpose of the business."

Otl Aicher calls places like this, where there has been successful cooperation, "workshops". They are not used for planning and administration, but for development and design. The design is guided towards the right result in a process of examination and correction. The principle of guidance by alternatives permits an exemplary start in something that already exists. Models of a "world as design" come into being.

Otl Aicher's writings are explorations of that world. They are a substantive part of his work. In moving through the history of thought and design, building and construction he assures the possibilities of arranging existence in a humane fashion. As ever he is concerned with the question of the conditions needed to produce a civilization culture. These conditions have to be fought for against apparent factual or material constraints and spiritual and intellectual substitute offers.

Otl Aicher has a taste for dispute. For this reason this volume contains polemical statements on cultural and political subjects as well as practical reports and historical exposition. Aicher fights with productive obstinacy above all for the renewal of Modernism, which he says has largely exhausted itself in aesthetic visions. He insists that the ordinary working day is still more important than "cultural sunday". But aesthetics can still not be reduced to art: "everything concrete, everything real, relates to aesthetics. art as pure aesthetics is even in danger of distracting attention from the aesthetic needs of the real world. there is no case in which there can be different aesthetic categories, a pure one and an everyday one. in moral terms we can also not distinguish between religious morality and the morality of every day."

Design as a way of life instead of cosmetic design: Otl Aicher trusts training of the senses. His life's work guarantees the fact that this trust remains modern.

insights can give you a shock. i had a shock like that on a visit to moscow in the mid seventies. i had been invited to discuss certain questions with the people responsible for the olympic games, which were to take place in moscow in 1980.

in this context i suggested that pioneering works of russian constructivism should be renovated, as visitors from the west were very interested in this architecture. i said that this architecture had been a crucial stimulus for the development of modern architecture.

i was met with incomprehension and rejection. this was still the period of "socialist realism", when painters were concerned to remain near to the people with superficial fidelity to nature and credible symbolism and gesture. this also means comprehensible to the simple worker, for the people. nikita khrushchev had already criticized stalin's wedding-cake style for being bombastic, decorative and uneconomical. stalin had had seven tower-like high-rise buildings put up around the centre of moscow as a sign of the victory over fascism, which like the famous moscow underground railway were decorated with feudal pomp and tarted up with bombastic drama, known to the people as the wedding-cake style. each tower was topped with a pointed spire with a red star on the top. the wedding-cake style fell prey to derision and irony and showed what happens when the state begins to worry about the cultural well-being and happiness of its citizens, which always basically leads to securing its power by giving out sweets.

khrushchev broke with the stalinist era and enjoyed laughing at obsessions with being a great man. but they were a long way away from bringing a non-representational painter like Malevich out of the cellar, as i recommended to the lady director of the tretiakov gallery, or remembering a russian architect like melnikov, who built the rusakov clubhouse, which is still stimulating today. natural and realistic behaviour was the order of the day, and they were still going to stay close to the people, but using a simpler approach.

I visited melnikov's domestic building that had once been epoch-making. melnikov was not only ostracized, he was intimidated and forgotten, and he was talked about behind people's hands. i would not have been admitted if a friend of his hadn't been standing outside the door with me.

this friend was in a position to show me all the buildings i had in mind when i suggested that the constructivists should be made accessible to the world. but gollosov's suyev clubhouse was in just as lamentable condition as ginsberg and milinis' narkomfin residential block and melinokov's rusakov clubhouse itself. even the trade union building le corbusier built in moscow was in a condition of intentional decay that made it impossible to look at only vesnin's pravda building and shchussev's lenin mausoleum had the good fortune to enjoy political goodwill.

along with berlin and new york, moscow was the most important city as far as 20th century cultural impetus to develop humane technology and to see science and technology becoming components of a new creative culture was concerned. moscow was an important melting pot for new ideas and approaches. this moscow was to be forgotten on command, the city transformed itself into a collection of neoclassical copies in white stucco.

of course one wonders how stalin was able to make the cultural rubbish of the wedding-cake style into an obligatory architectural doctrine by state decree and forbid architecture that consciously subscribed to technology and industrial manufacture in the way that socialism wanted to humanize technology and industry over all. at first one tends to think that stalin got this from hitler. speer's neoclassicism was gigantic and bombastic, and the gesture of the sculptures by artists like thorak and breker that were placed upon it was dramatically overblown and stilted. the nuremberg buildings gave an idea of how german cities were to be rebuilt after the war, if the war were to be won: monumental, overladen and overproportioned.

but then the discovery was made, and it was this that was akin to a shock, that it was not stalin enforcing his taste here, but the so-called modern architects themselves. there is a design by ginsburg for a theatre in novosibirsk dating from 1931 that is all constructivist functionality. but five years later ginsburg built this theatre in a style of highly academic classicism.

what had happened? ginsburg himself had become convinced that the masses did not understand the new constructivist architecture. ginsburg was not only one of the most successful constructivist architects, he was also the movement's theoretician. the man who had brought le corbusier to moscow developed an artistic theory according to which all styles start simply, but that they cannot be tolerated in their simple form; they become decorative, until finally they go under in a kind of baroque overload, this means that ginsburg, just like all bourgeois art theoreticians, thought in stylistic and formal terms, he started with aesthetics. in the end he did not think at all constructively and functionally, technology was just a new formal repertory, a material at the artist's disposal, a new sign language, a new zeitgeist that was being used.

i went into the moscow museum of architecture and asked to see ginsburg's drawings and had to admit, shakily: it was the modern movement itself that brought all the historical kitsch back from the rubbish dump. and i discovered that ginsburg was interpreting modernism formalistically as early as 1923. his books were called: *rhythm in architecture* and *style and epoch.*

i was myself staying in a hotel that shchussev had built about 1934, already with the first classical profiles and cornices, in concrete at first, later they had to be executed in natural stone. at first it was still restrained classicism, profiling of surface using pilaster cornices and window borders followed the rules of suprematism as developed by malevich in his spatial models.

there were also individual designers in the west who started off as pioneers of a new kind of design, but then collapsed under the third reich. the creator of the new typography, jan tschichold, forgot himself and finally worshipped at the altar of the new classicism, which soon turned out to be prestigious enough to guarantee the new dictators an appropriate display of power. mussolini too was in sympathy with futurism at first, but later he found himself better accommodated in a copy of roman antiquity than in a building with a rational basis.

i was familiar with western examples but the fact that almost the whole russian avant-garde gave up their experiment themselves, in order to chum up with state monumentalism, did come as a shock, and gave me a great deal to think about.

in the meantime i have got cleverer. i see in so-called post-modern architects the same escape into an historicizing style, into styleaesthetics, into formal composition, into symbolism, into aesthetic myth. what has been forgotten is this century's attempt to reconcile technology with human beings, by opening ourselves up to it. refuge is taken in style, in metaphysical aesthetics, in form, in historical models, in quotation. palladio is the most quoted architect, even if he is built in steel and glass.

18

the hard years of the industrial revolution, the civil war, collectivization and industrialization were obviously so burdensome in terms of internal politics that the people was offered the kind of art it liked. that is, or so it is thought, the art of palaces, of splendour and of gold, art for art's sake, decoration for decorations. this is then at the same time the art of the state, with which the state makes visible its existence as power and superior power. the people, so it is believed, needs adoration.

in a similar way we are also served with the enjoyment of life today. the post-war period is over, the revolution of '68 is over, the period of social movements is over. we set ourselves up in beauty itself, even if we are suffocating in rubbish and the world is falling apart. gone are the utopias of a new society, new education, new ways of getting on with each other, new relationships between the sexes, gone are the movements for a life without death by chemicals, for food without additives, for natural nature. we are back to spraying our hair with cfc's and all the colours of the rainbow. we wear things that make us look good and for a service society the greatest services are those of beautification, styling and design. we have come to live in a society of design for superficial covering.

design and architecture are in a profound crisis. they are in danger of becoming the dogsbodies of fashions. they are no longer derived from argument and good reasons like science and technology, but from whim, from aesthetic chance, according to which art can be worshipped and cannibalized.

this is to a large extent caused by the fact that there is no profession concerned with the theory and history of design, in the way that the art historian has his firm place in present-day culture and science. the industrial archaeologist, the man who deals with the history of technology and technological theory is not yet part of our academic establishment. and therefore building orientated towards design and technology has no intellectual accompaniment or analytical presentation. the few exceptions only confirm the state of affairs. in goethe's day artistic beauty was discovered alongside natural beauty and art historians were appointed to look after it. design beauty, technological beauty has not yet been discerned, and so no theoretician of technical artefacts has been appointed.

it has turned out to be disastrous that the theory of design and architecture is looked after by art historians. design is quite different from art. design and art are

related in the same way as knowledge and faith. there may
be scientists who are religious. but in principle science
is different from religion.

design must rest on the same foundations as science
and technology. it too draws life from argument. art and
metaphysics lie beyond argument. here statements are
made, rather than reasons given. even though st. thomas
aquinas says that faith and knowledge cannot contradict
each other, faith is still so subjective that it is possible to
believe anything that does not represent a contradiction.
essentially there are as many religions as there are
individuals.

design relates to states of affairs, it is related to language. language too is worth as much as its ability to
reproduce states of affairs. its achievement lies in also
being able to reproduce those states of affairs that it has
so far not exoressed. its yardstick is its sureness of aim.
attempts to handle language without content as in
abstract art may be assumed to be doomed to failure.

design consists of developing products appropriately to
their factual content. and above all this means adapting
to new states of affairs. in a changing world, products
must change as well.

but what is the measure of design, new states of
affairs or art? today design has gone downhill and
degenerated into applied art.

post-modernism is a new faith. it is not design, but a
kind of religion or, as it defines itself, dedicated to myth.
what myth? the myth of the 20th century, the myth of
archetypes, the myth of prehistoric social structures? one
may choose between c.g. jung and claude lévistrauss and
should not be surprised to arrive at Alfred Rosenberg and
his way of shaping the world. there is no bridge of reason from the architecture of post-modernism to the noe-
classicism of stalin and hitler, no bridge of argument,
though there probably is a bridge of myth. mussolini's
relapse from futurism into the architecture of ancient
rome is the way of myth, and corresponds with leon
krier's relapse into a film city made up of old bits of
scenery.

it is not possible to quarrel about myth. but it is possible to quarrel about design, just as it is possible to
quarrel about science, technology, about economics and
politics, about everything that drives the modern world
and holds it together and forces it apart. design must
have its reasons.

i know that many people cannot accept this. magnago
lampugnani says that today chairs are close to being

20

works of art. and that for this reason a certain amount of discomfort has to be put up with. at any other time this would have been seen as pure nonsense, drivel. in our pluralistic society thinking seems to have become pluralistic as well, uncritical, conformist, balanced. the little two-times-table has been replaced by the great not only but also.

a chair that is not good to sit on is not a good chair. perhaps it can become a work of art if it is hung on the wall, where it doesn't actually belong, or can be a psychic stage prop. it will never be good design.

it is clear that the simplest states of affairs have been displaced, distorted, disjointed, dismembered, destroyed. it does not seem to suit thinking, particularly thinking about simple states of affairs, if it withdraws into myth and sees the phenomenon as a symbol.

today there is no homeric laughter, no homeric mockery, otherwise a new philosophy like this would be swept away by the breath from the roars of laughter that the programme caused. no, we carry on solemnly sitting on an uncomfortable chair, even when it is only a work of art in embryo.

a chair that is not good to sit on is a bad chair, even if it would be suitable as a work of art. it is bad design.

a statement of this kind has rarity value nowadays. anyone who argues the other way round, and says precisely that today chairs are on their way to becoming works of art and that as a consequence a certain amount of discomfort has to be put up with, is made the new director of the frankfurt museum of architecture (like magnago lampugnani).

the former director, art historian heinrich klotz, has now been appointed to set up a new centre for modern media, art and design in karlsruhe. this was commissioned by lothar späth, the regional prime minister with the brightest ideas, who wanted to give his land a "new future". lothar späth has read the signs of the times. while franz josef strauss wanted to give his land new economic input with nuclear energy, nuclear science, nuclear technology, and a new industrial estate from oberpfaffenhofen, ottobrunn, wackersdorf to erlangen, lothar späth has climbed a storey higher, and arrived at silicon valley, computers and computer art.

both land prime ministers have cocked a snook at the liberal state with its market economy and introduced economic policy, research policy and cultural policy as mercantile planning and control elements. to the good of their citizens. however, they both asserted that they had no time for state intervention, and lothar späth said that nothing was more stupid than a politician trying to get involved with culture. neither franz josef strauss nor lothar späth was directly involved in cultural, research or economic policy as such, but they distributed the funds, the subsidies, every mark and every pfennig, that the public purse makes available for culture, business, science and research. is this not planning and direction?

a year after his death, the policies of franz josef strauss, with the end of wackersdorf, are a graveyard. that's how quickly mercantilism runs against its own walls. nobel prizewinner mößbauer, the bought-in advertisement for new research in bavaria, would rather have left the country anyway.

lothar späth remained as prince in residence. he gave complete freedom to culture, economics, research, as he had said. but there was money for those people who produced the culture, the business and the science that the father of the land wanted.

this made lothar späth the caring father of everything that was happening in the land. he made the culture, he made the business, he made the research, just as every princely house determines the well-being of its people. it was the dukes of württemberg and the electors and margraves of baden who built the palaces of ludwigsburg, stuttgart, solitude, mannheim and karlsruhe, and who encouraged the commercial zeal that made the allemanic lands into flourishing industrial states.

this may all be an historical swindle, as it was the craftsmen, the cities, the guilds who produced a flourishing country, before it was brought down by absolutism. the princes raised taxes and squandered them on buildings and other things, then had to sell the sons of their soil for cash to foreign rulers as cannon fodder. and yet this pattern, let us say "flourishing baroque", is still the model for modern culture in this country.

culture in baden-württemberg is state culture. two examples:

one is ulm and the closure of the private hochschule für gestaltung by the state. the other is the new art and media centre in karlsruhe, also a state initiative.

lothar späth said himself that it was he who closed the hochschule für gestaltung in ulm, although it was on behalf of filbinger, the then prime minister and hahn, his minister of culture.

unfortunately the school acquired an international reputation with hindsight. it could no longer be covered up by intentional forgetfulness. lothar späth even went as far as to say that closing this school was one of the most stupid things he had ever done. he went even further, and said he would like to found a successor institution. at least this is how the centre for art and media technology that is being established in karlsruhe sees itself.

heinrich klotz, who is responsible for this centre, says:

"the dessau bauhaus and the hochschule für gestaltung in ulm can serve as models. the bauhaus was the first to direct art from the craftsman to the machine. the hochschule für gestaltung in ulm continued the work of the bauhaus by combining art and industrial products. the centre for art and media technology relates the arts to digital techniques, appropriately to the possibilities of the late 20th century."

as far as ulm is concerned this is just plain wrong. the opposite is the case. the reputation and working results of the hochschule für gestaltung are not based on combining, but on separating art and industry. we refused to have artists' studios. lack of prior training meant that artists and art were not in a position to influence industrial civilization. we had to develop a new view of a new, technically orientated design, design that could think from technology for technology, and that was competent enough to use its knowledge of products, technical procedures, manufacturing processes and economic organization to bring about more humane design of industrial products, better social acceptability and enhanced usefulness. you could ask art about this through the length and breadth of the land, but it wouldn't be able to come up with an answer. it is interested in the next world, not this one.

heinrich klotz is an art historian. it does not say much for his academic methods when he states the precise opposite of what was actually the case. there was no artistic model for the design of braun radios and electric equipment. there was no artistic model for the corporate identity of lufthansa or the munich olympics. on the contrary, whenever anyone said that there were general artistic criteria for design, we had to go our separate ways. we thought things out from the matter itself. many of the teachers had originally worked as artists for a time, but their life experience was precisely the opposite: art is not suitable for purpose-directed design work. it only gets in the way.

consequently it is possible to say even now that the painters who are now intended to use new digital techniques will very soon abandon their computers because they do not know how to use them. i have enough practical experience with computers myself to know how difficult it is to use them when you want creativity from them. the swabians, who are not bad technicians and not bad workers, call them "blechesel" - tin donkeys. tin donkeys because you have to tell them everything they have to do and because they only listen to people who speak their language.

a designer must be at home in the categories of technology and science. syllabuses in the hochschule für gestaltung in ulm were models for new concepts of responsible handling of technology and its moral and cultural mastery. here painting was definitely too little, and it was not possible to hold a conversation with an engineer or an economist on the basis of aesthetic sensibilities. even the aesthetic dimension had to be developed from use and technology.

all right, this school no longer exists. it was strangled, closed, just as the bauhaus had been closed thirty years before. then by a dictatorship, now by a democracy. but it is quite impossible, without demonstrating one's own lack of understanding, to take it over as a centre for art and media technology with an integrated design school. ulm would be a warning.

modernism developed, and this is perhaps most clearly seen in the works of the engineers of the last century, from uninhibited handling of technology as an open system. this concept was fully demonstrated by the crystal palace in london, built by joseph paxton in 1851. art itself was not involved in this, at that time it was clinging to copying historic models, which was an embarrassing rather than a creative process.

this attitude of modernism is seen again in constructivism, although technology was often material that could be used expressively for art in this case. this is visible again today in the buildings of rogers, foster and hopkins, who cite buckminster fuller, prouvé and wachsmann. modernism has integrated technolgy, it can be defined as a creative expression of technology even in its responsibility to human society.

to come back to the chair. a modern chair in this sense can only be a structurally intelligent chair, a chair that is cleanly thought through in terms of manufacturing technology, showing the criteria of scientific ergonomics.

but this chair can only be designed by someone with the technical perceptions of a charles eames, who put as much hard thought into his work as a surgeon does for

24

an operation. visions are not enough here, they can even be harmful, however artistic they may be.

the crisis of modernism lies in the fact that thought and criteria concerned with making are replaced by an aesthetic vision.

a vision of this kind produces a chair made of a mixture of "up-to-date" materials like perforated metal, beech wood and plastic, brightly painted, a spectacular object, but not very nice to sit on. this would bring us back to the motto of the new wave, which admittedly is a fashion like every other wave; objects become art, life becomes art.

the relationship of art and technology is irreversible. technology has a technical beauty of its own. but the reverse is not true, art does not have a technical dimension. the material technical significance of a van gogh is precisely zero in comparison with its artistic value or even its value on the art market, quite apart from the fact that contemporary art has started to use cheap material, rubbish and scrap as a protest. we are dealing with two worlds here, one that is not interested in technology and one that processes

functioning technology aesthetically. a computer used for artistic purposes does not have to achieve anything and produces as many aesthetic structures as you like, but they are always the ones that you put in.

a sculpture that achieves something is no longer a work of art but a machine or a device, and its aesthetics relate to its use. but art wishes to eschew mere effect.

art is syntax without semantics. it has nothing to say. otherwise it would be a piece of information. it is closer to being a symbol than a statement. it is devoted to redundancy. and anyone who attempts when faced with this state of affairs to transfer art to technology ends up with icing, whether of the stalinist kind or the postmodernist persuasion.

art moves in the realm of the symbol. a circle, a square is interpreted symbolically by Kandinsky, and so are the colours red, green or blue. outside the world of the symbol a piece of felt or a piece of margarine would be felt or margarine. in art it is meant to be something different. perhaps this is what we call zeitgeist, something higher in other words, that makes us think of hegel's "weltgeist", or world spirit. it is just that we have become suspicious of world-reason. truth lies within a thing, not above it.

i interpret the crisis of modernism like this: the ingenious constructivism of the 19th century, documented by names like paxton, eiffel or maillart, has been overtaken by art and seized, monopolized. this dominance by art is a contradiction. it would not exist if there were not authorities able to play politics with this kind of aesthetic metaphysics, cultural politics, but still robust interest politics, state policy to secure the status quo.

the world is in a strange condition. we discover that our forests are dying, do all we can to prevent it, and it continues to increase. we discover atmospheric pollution, we do all we can to prevent it, and contamination continues to increase. we discover a hole in the ozone layer, we forbid the use of hydrofluorocarbons and the hole in the ozone layer gets bigger and bigger. we produce any quantity of rubbish and poisonous by-products, we do all we can to prevent it, but grow mountains of poison and rubbish that we can scarcely get rid of any more. we try to reduce carbon dioxide emissions, but global warming increases. we burn dioxin containers and the minister of the environment resignedly discovers that everything is contaminated with dioxin.

design should be called for here, as we are talking about products that are exclusively produced by man. design should be called for here that is critical, that can question things, that is analytical and can uncover roots. instead design is constantly encouraged by the state as a way of making even more beautiful packaging, of stoking consumption with even more products that nobody wants, of making the surface of things that are often superficial even more brightly coloured and attractive and of reducing existence to merely working our way through constantly changing fashions. the state is interested in a contented, tranquil society and in the sort of icing-sugar culture with which power has always tried to get out of critical situations. the more dubious the state of the world becomes, the more beautiful it is to be. there have never been so many museums built as there are today, shrines of transcendent aesthetics.

the state can always find someone to fight alongside it. there is money available. no individual can found a school today. all design schools, all architecture schools, belong to the state. it pays all their teachers, it approves all their courses. it pays for all their buildings and equipment. it has its say in the most fundamental way, without even needing to raise its little finger. design degenerates, runs the official definition, into sales promotion. it becomes the elixir of consumerism in an information society. design centres shoot out of the ground one after the other.

we are experiencing culture being ruined by state
monopoly. the state does not even have to make an
effort to make its influence felt. the fact that it fills the
feeding troughs has tamed even the wildest beasts. the
citizens are domesticated once and for all. the state
pours out the wine of patronage.

the state destroyed my youth. i was twelve when hitler
came to power. the state destroyed the hochschule für
gestaltung, and i was one of its founders. this was under
a democracy that sees itself as representative, a führer
democracy.

the state is destroying a critical and analytical culture
before our very eyes and creativity is degenerating to the
manufacture of beautiful façades and beautiful packaging. the show has to be even more colourful. the principle of progress means increasing turnover by ever more
beautiful consumption.

mercantilism in this country is culturally as active as
the builders of palaces of ludwigsburg, the solitude or
karlsruhe. the state has been seized by a baroque building frenzy. everywhere it is building the new temples of
edification, museums. modernism is finding its way back
to buckled shoes and wigs, to silk, hooped skirt and pow-
der, to a new corporate identity, to a new culture of surface and superficiality. we have bread, we have circuses.

we feel better than ever before, however loudly the
clock is ticking. enjoyment is the content of life. the
hands and face of the clock are getting so smart and so
pretty that we can't read them any more, because we are
not intended to read them any more. that is what modernism has to do today. stop us finding out what the bell
is tolling.

doing without symbols

numerous german towns and cities are trying hard to put up memorials to deserters in the world wars. i cannot summon up any enthusiasm for this. people think that because i wrote an anti-war book, a deserter's book, that i would be for the idea. i don't even really know why i am so sceptical about monuments and memorials for the victims of national socialism. auschwitz is beyond memorials.

i advised someone working in the neuengamme concentration camp museum to replace symbols with information and symbolic memorials with elucidation.

everyone should know what the people in concentration camps had to eat, what work they had to do, how they lived together, how they were treated, what punishments there were, what legitimacy, how high the death rate was. the cooler information of this kind is, the less memorial rituals slip in, the more powerful it will be. fact is more powerful than interpretation.

there used to be monuments to the german kaiser in all german cities. they have disappeared. no-one would know the difference between a kaiser wilhelm the first and a kaiser wilhelm the second any more.

there are still bismarck monuments standing. even a social-democratic chancellor or the publisher of a german news magazine can be an admirer of bismarck. it is precisely here that we see where replacing information with symbols takes you.

the germans ought to know more about bismarck. they ought to know that the prussian defence budget was seven times higher than france's, that bismarck quite consciously saw his political approach as one of blood and iron, they ought to know how he held democrats up to ridicule, they ought to know how systematically he set out to seize territory, how he overran peaceful towns and countries. they ought to know that he was one of the outstanding politicians of violence, the might of the stronger, the politics of fear. bismarck did not become the famed master of realpolitik until he had everything he wanted and had to tell himself that he would be bending the bow too far if he went any further.

bismarck hides behind his figure. and so german historians do not dare to touch bismarck as a topic. the symbol hides it. the monument distorts reality.

certainly symbols are more than knowledge in german thought. the world that cannot be fathomed rationally appears in the symbol. the unsayable becomes manifest. no enlightenment managed to shake the role, the position of the symbol in the hierarchy of thinking in germany. we have remained devout, even in politics.

in france, marianne as a symbol of the grande nation is an allegory. but an allegory is not a symbol, it is an image, a comparison, a circumscription. and human communication is based on images. images are often more precise than scientific definitions.

there is much that cannot be described or grasped rationally. not everything that is is reasonable and not everything that is reasonable is real. the identification of reason and reality is inadmissible in principle because rational definition is a product of culture, just as the division of the earth into degrees is a product of culture that does not occur in nature. knowledge is created. thus a great deal that is remains outside knowledge. the only question is, does it remain in principle outside that which can be grasped rationally, and thus always outside, or is it simply still undiscovered.

for the french, who are still in the tradition of the enlightenment, it is still inaccessible. for the germans there is a knowledge that is above rationality. it appears in symbols. it appears in faith and it appears in art. religion and art are irrational, they are symbols. will, nietzsche's will, will in history. will in politics is also irrational. it appears in symbols. it appears in the image of the antichrist, the superman, the lord of castle and palace, in war and in triumphal arches, in parades and imperial party conferences.

there are fundamental experiences of reality, there are fundamental experiences of one's own ego that are not at the disposal of the rational. we turn to the image. language has hundreds of images for the state of the heart, from stonehearted to chickenhearted. but here the image remains information, like the definition as well. pictorial statement and scientific statement are on the same plane, are contingent upon each other. they want to be precise, even if by different means.

symbols are something else for germans. the symbol opens up other worlds. it makes being accessible and opens up the actual. symbols have depth, reality is only there. all any ruler can do in a monument is sit on a horse. there has never been one who has sat on an ass.

bismarck stands there as an upright figure, leaning on a sword that comes up to his chest. he has the figure of a knight, and yet he destroyed the old empire, a man of campaigns and raids, who threw the former leaders of austria out of the imperial club in order to secure the predominance of prussia, a predominance that was to be rich in consequence.

a cult of symbols broke out. in germany the concept of metaphysics was shifted to the great and deep hereafter, to which no path of reason led. metaphysics is what cannot be grasped, only interpreted. metaphysics is apprehension between life and death, is apprehension of the reason for the world. böcklin, also an admirer of bismarck, created the metaphysical painting "the isle of the dead", which it is not difficult to recognize as a symbolic vagina. in an age of victorian morality, where one cannot speak about such things, it is for this area in particular that symbols tend to shoot out of the ground.

german metaphysics works on the basis that the world is governed by a spiritual principle. here it is in the tradition of Greek philosophy. but this spiritual principle, whether idea or world-reason, is distorted by facts. for this reason knowledge of facts can be an obstacle to discovering the world-reason. we need cognition that goes beyond reason. and this cognition manifests itself in the symbol. thus germans are not content with living in a state and organizing this state according to their needs and ideas, they need a fatherland that is so great that they are also prepared to offer their lives for it. it is only this fatherland as a higher essence that gives meaning, gives direction, to their lives. in the fatherland history's demands become effective.

working for a state that guarantees the best possible life for all its citizens is too little for the germans. history itself, according to hegel and marx as well, is world revolution.

in the mean time the french have also discovered the symbol in their own way. this in the form of symbolic existence and symbolic action. structuralism is the discovery of the symbolic in history and society. we do not do what we want but what we should. we are driven by a hidden structure, a codex of customs and prescriptions. the meaning of the actual has a higher meaning. and this gives the higher meaning the possibility, as in postmodernism, of replacing the actual.

the door is replaced by the portal. even in the country, family houses are built with portals, framed by a column on each side and a pediment. the columns may not have doric, ionic or corinthian capitals any more, they are derived from the formal language of the bauhaus. but they represent a symbolic, a representative existence. whether the column bears a load or not is of no importance.

the romans, who originally built in brick, took the column over from the greeks. they were concerned to look not just like lords of the state or lords of war, but like lords of educational distinction. banks and stock exchanges in the last century took over columns from the romans. no-one wanted to present himself as a mere businessman or factory owner, and so the classical column was used as a sign of culture and education, whether it was cribbed from the romans themselves or its more recent renaissance version.

the modern column is smooth as a pipe, without base or fluting, but it is no less a sign of higher things. it goes beyond function, purpose, rational definition, justification in reason, it is a pointer to history and culture. it is a quotation. it maintains a dialogue with the architecture of yesteryear. at the same time it shows solidarity with the conservative bourgeoisie of the last century. post-modernism is a modern justification of the historicism with which conservative society camouflaged its business.

we too have business to camouflage. big business has turned out to result in poisoning nature and the environment, excessive consumption has turned out to produce rubbish and trash. our wonderful mobility has turned out to be something that blocks up our streets and is the meaning of frustration when on holiday. the comfort of new furniture is the fruit of an artificial wood whose manufacture produces gases that make the forests die.

the class struggle, ruinous competition, manchester capitalism, the exploitation of the weak took place in the 19th century among the symbols of humanistic education, before a background of neoclassical architecture. the consequences of excessive consumption require a similar concern with education, historical awareness, classical aesthetics and openness to the world.

the world needs symbols. thus art is flourishing as almost never before, as in the courts of princes. museums are being built almost as never before, and the works of the poor impressionist and expressionist painters find their way into the vaults not of the state, but of insurance companies and concerns that are taking a cut of the new prosperity.

art is what cannot be understood. if you understand what a picture is showing then it is no longer art. thus art turns away from all forms of the comprehensible, it turns towards the actual domain of the irrational, towards aesthetics as such.

religion used to be belief in a doctrine, in a revealed truth. today religion is belief in religiousness as such, in religiousness in any form, in the appearance of the world as symbol. art used to be the ability to represent something. art today is the aesthetic of the unrepresented, the aesthetic of aesthetics itself. the picture of what is depicted becomes the symbol of what cannot be depicted.

warlords spoke of nothing more frequently than peace. nothing concerns the head of a company, other than his business, more than art. man as a symbolic existence is the prerequisite of a society that no longer lives on what it needs but consumes what is produced. consumption itself has to be given symbolic value.

the social state once wanted to abolish poverty. the welfare state came into being. at the moment we are in the act of abandoning even this again. we are turning things round. we fatten ourselves up with excess production. growth must grow. we are moving from need consumption to the consumption of symbols.

it seems that this calculation has worked out. an advertisement for one of the biggest car manufacturers quotes goethe: kunst bleibt kunst, art remains art. it does not tell us anything about the car, its performance, what it costs. such figures could be alarming. it also offers no information about the relationship between car and environment. it raises the car to the status of art, makes it into a higher idea. anyone who drives a car lives in the lofty places of the west.

a distinction has to be made between symbol and sign. human culture is one of signs. even material was translated into signs, into weight and mass, into mark and pfennig. signs stand for something, point to a thing or a set of circumstances. a symbol wants more. it reaches beyond the thing. it looks behind it.

a sign cannot offer more than an equivalent to a thing and state of affairs. a symbol tries to remove this distinction, wants to look behind things. it is not content with truth as correspondence between signs, statement and state of affairs.

admittedly, no truth is exhaustive. behind every answer there is a question. but can we, instead of asking more questions, do without answers and be content with seeming and appearance? in fact not just be content, but seek the real truth precisely in this, in seeming?

the world is turning upside down. ultimately it is all appearance. only an appearance of appearances. things vanish anyway. things used to have to be manufactured.

today they come from the factory, made by automization and robots. work is no longer the manufacture of things. this means that the experience of making is lost. knowledge becomes theoretical knowledge. appearance now takes the place of experience. things are no longer designed. design is stuck on to them retrospectively. as design in inverted commas, as form of appearance, as a symbol. things no longer have a purpose to fulfil, they are produced for us to consume. they exist in terms of the meaning we put on them, they have symbolic value.

the prospect that a car could turn back into a vehicle again today is very slight, however. any objective representation of cars, traffic and its consequences would be tantamount to condemnation. and no-one can afford that, neither the manufacturers nor the politicians, who think in national economic dimensions, and certainly not the customer, who has been offered a taste of an alleged new freedom by the car. he believes in this freedom, even when he is stuck in a jam several miles long. symbolic use of things presupposes belief in symbols. and anyone who believes in symbols rescues the economy of symbols.

our civilization drives us out of every kind of work, whether it be manufacturing things, picking fruit or carrying out services. the only work that is of real economic use is that done by machines, automated devices and robots. people's own work is a disruptive factor in the modern national economy. it is getting closer to black market work. the only sphere of activity left to human beings is that of making decisions. decisions at the computer, decisions in offices.

in this way we lose our relationship with things and affairs, our understanding of cause and effect, of plan and result. all reasons and purposes, all causalities and relations are fleeing from our world.

what remains is enjoyment.

enjoyment comes in two forms, first as physiological satisfaction and then as mental satisfaction. the symbol is to be, say, as strong as schwarzenegger or as clever as al capone or as successful as frank sinatra. and not the symbol as a sign, but as a dream, as transcendence. arno schmidt thought that in a future world there would be nothing left but surfaces, no essence of things any more. in the mean time we have already taken it a little further. we no longer buy things because of their appearance, because of their form, we buy them as symbols. they no longer represent themselves, but what has been breathed into them as transcendence. economy today is the manufacture of secular transcendence, the production of dreams.

woe betide anyone who still talks about the actual, who talks about purposes and functions, who talks about sense and nonsense. he will not get a foothold in the market, unless he is in a position to create his own market.

nothing is itself any more. everything points to something else, has to be like that and this. a chair isn't a chair any more. it has to look like a sculpture, like a work of art.

otherwise no market growth can be guaranteed. otherwise no additional purchasing power can be generated. otherwise there will be no more expansion of production. otherwise there will be no growth in the gross national product. the symbol guarantees power of disposal over the market, over the consumer. the transcendence of control manifests itself in the symbol.

that is one world. the other is that in fact we are destroying symbol after symbol. since woodstock all the scenery is burning. stage sets consist of scaffolding and spotlights. light as appearance, as the mood of the here-after has gone out. simulation of sunset and the twilight of the gods has glowed into darkness. light is electric light. it comes out of spotlights that you can see. staging the hereafter has been replaced by technical hardware and its operational use as a game. a spotlight produces a beam of light, a colour filter produces coloured light, a dimmer creates light and dark, and miniature motors produce rotation. and all that before the eyes of the assembled public. nothing is "hidden".

one is reminded of a marionette theatre that is all the more convincing the more you can see the strings and operating bars. one is reminded of bach, for whom music consisted of sounds.

what is, one is permitted to see. that too is a message of our century, the second, if the first was: nothing is real, everything is a symbol. what is, one is permitted to see is a principle that does not allow anything to be taboo any more and penetrates into the holy of holies of power mechanisms, into the secret storehouse of the practice of power.

a spotlight is a structure made of metal cylinders, of cones, a mirror, a lamp, screws, holders and fasteners. one is permitted to see it.

the light that it produces is different from natural light. it is technical light, not sunlight, light from a bulb. since the invention of the spotlight we have had

34

earth-bound light, light without symbolic value. light, once the symbol of metaphysical twilight, has become a manufactured technical medium. the aura of the symbol is glowing into darkness. richard wagner, the master of metaphysical light and metaphysical music, is being carried away by the electric engineer.

aesthetic existence

everybody cooks what he plants, says a mexican proverb. translated for european conditions it could mean something like, everybody thinks what he makes. and what does a bank clerk make, or an economist, or an official in the federal statistics department, or a spares manager at BMW, or a genetic researcher for la roche in basle? he operates a computer.

what does a european make today? he doesn't make anything any more, he makes decisions. he sits in front of his screen and if the computer doesn't know anything else and offers this or that possibility the european says let's try it this way, then that. something will work.

we do not craft our own furniture any more, we don't sing our own songs any more, we don't dig our own gardens any more, we don't make our own toys any more, we don't cook our own soup and food any more, we don't write our own letters any more, we don't clean our own rooms any more, we even get rid of our own communication.

everything comes from the refrigerator, the television, the self-service shop. in this way man has probably achieved the most difficult of all difficult existences. he no longer needs to work, he no longer needs to think, he no longer needs to make anything, he is free. all he has to do is switch on programmes.

but the human in the human being cannot be suppressed. nothing is more important to him than his real freedom. he is himself through selfdetermination. but what can he determine when there is nothing left to be determined? something that is indeterminate. that is aesthetic phenomena.

no-one can stop me wearing a moustache like kaiser wilhelm the second. no-one can stop me wearing a tailcoat like stresemann, no-one can stop me keeping my hat on while eating, no-one can stop me painting pictures in which all the people are standing on their heads.

the realm of freedom is increasingly being reduced to the realm of aesthetics, and there all freedoms are allowed. in aesthetics there are no bans, no standards, no rules. something that is posited as an aesthetic fact exists, is legitimate, is legal, is inevitable, is there.

thus today true human existence is aesthetic existence.

so far, so good. but now the question arises: which aesthetic do i set for myself, which do i choose, which do i slip into. let us leave aside the fact that many slip into the aesthetic of the beach boys or of udo lindenberg or of mother theresa or of madonna or of karl lagerfeld or katherine hamnett. everybody lives on orientations and objectifications. one assesses oneself while assessing others.

the aesthetic that one chooses oneself is not only a problem for the individual person, making one's own aptitudes and talents agree with something objective. today aesthetics shows which class you belong to.

communism, socialism, we read in the paper every day, is finished. we live in a classless society. probably true. reason enough to rediscover class, to set class up again. not economic classes this time, this time aesthetic classes, representative classes.

economic classes had crude distinctive features: wages, honorarium, salary, the monthly income. this alone distinguished capitalists from the proletariat. the distinguishing mark of the new classes is more sublime. it is based on the choice of aesthetic.

an example: a football trainer is usually somewhat older than his players, because he is more experienced. in training he kicks the ball around in the same tracksuit as them. he must not play worse than his pupils, but it is agreed that he probably wouldn't last through a whole game any longer.

during a game the trainer sits on the reserve bench with his substitutes. now the game of aesthetics begins. one trainer sits there dressed the same as his players. the other doesn't sit, but stands, and he doesn't wear a sports top, but a jacket, and he doesn't have training shoes, but elegant street shoes, and he doesn't have an open neck, but a tie or bow tie. his trousers have creases, which no sports trousers have. his shirt is buttoned up, the opposite of what sportsmen usually go for. his trousers are tight-fitting, something taboo in sport.

sport was a revolution against common decency. you didn't play in jacket and plus-fours, but in vest and underpants. this has led to the casual colourful world of strips that is appropriate to the game and also practically made it possible in the first place.

a team manager cannot be involved in this, it would be the wrong aesthetic for him. he needs a jacket and tie. he needs shoes and trouser creases. why?

because only someone who can afford to wear useless, impractical, unsporting things while others are wearing things that are useful, practical and sporting has authority.

the aesthetic of the fine man was always the aesthetic of the impractical, the purposeless, the unmotivated, the functionless.

it is only possibly to make oneself distinct from the world of purpose and order by nonsense, or putting it somewhat more modestly, by not-sense, by senselessness.

that is why functionalism has been pronounced dead and buried today. things that are sensible, purposeful, useful, reasonable have no place in the class of the sublime. in them the opposite is true. the manager, the director, the chairman and the representative only identify themselves by demonstrating how unreasonable they are, whether it be in their dress, their homes, their cars or even their thinking.

why stand around on the wet grass of a football stadium in town shoes that are only suitable for walking from the car to the office? why be the only person in the stadium with a buttoned shirt?

that man has authority. he stands above the matter in hand. he may well say: it was the players' fault, when a game is lost, and when the players have won a game he says that they followed his strategy. even now we don't really know: who is playing football, the players or the coach? it is clear from appearance, from aesthetic existence.

you have to know how to make an exhibition of yourself. art has always made an exhibition of itself. today the following conclusion is drawn from this: anyone who makes an exhibition of himself is making art, is a work of art. only what is different is striking.

this is the real reason for the present-day liaison between art and business. the only person who can do business is the one who is as different as art.

art is the domain of the completely different. what is normal is not art. what is sensible isn't art either. art is legitimized by the claim always to do everything differently. anyone who paints in the way that people have always painted is unoriginal.

for a time there was an attempt to combine the creative with the useful, the creative with the reasonable. it was thought that useful things could be well made and look good as well. like a training shoe or a bicycle. those days seem to have gone. design too is concerned today to make art or at least to convey art. design today consists of making structures that look as though they are by dalí, mondrian or kandinsky. you can't sit on a modern chair, it isn't there for sitting on. it contributes to the aesthetic ambience with which one demonstrates one's superiority.

conversely, anyone who wants to demonstrate superiority, who doesn't want to be like the others, has to become involved with art. no manager today can afford not to understand art. no concern can afford not to support art.

of course we all know that the world is different. if aeroplanes were built according to aesthetic criteria of whim they would all drop out of the sky. if engines were constructed according to aesthetic criteria they would never run, if traffic regulations were made according to aesthetic criteria there would not be any more traffic. because there is consistency, the world is legality and reason, even walls would not remain standing if they were not built functionally, skyscrapers would fall down if they were not constructed according to calculations and logic, and all soup would burn if it was cooked according to aesthetic criteria alone. reason and functionality are nothing more than insights into the way in which the world works. and this totally and completely. nature knows no aesthetic opposed to reason.

we all know that. nevertheless people do have an aesthetic existence, a form of existence that is against purpose and reason. and this has probably always existed. two hundred years ago the man standing on the grass was not wearing a tie and trousers with creases but buckled shoes and a wig. the man of privilege, the important man in the absolutist state, the nobleman, the king, the emperor showed himself in the size of his artificial wig. and the highest of all was the man who was condemned to inactivity by his wig, because otherwise it would have dropped off his head.

the more distinctive a power is, the more aesthetic extravagance it develops. this is the same in the case of the dome of st. peter's as it is for the hall of mirrors in versailles or the moscow underground. the greater the despot, the more beautiful the world becomes.

it used to be said that knowledge is power. in very early times they might have said: ability is power. today we say: beauty is power. only someone who can offer beauty has a chance of dominating the market. only someone who has slipped into an aesthetic existence has leadership qualities.

admittedly this will only be true for as long as aesthetic is understood as something beyond purpose and rational explanation.

zeitgeist, the spirit of the age, is a concept that particularly suits the spirit of the age. spirit is the highest, the spirit of the age the deepest. but if common notions are usually commonplaces, then zeitgeist turns out to be particularly imprecise. anyone is entitled to understand it as he formulates it.

zeitgeist is an invention of bourgeois art history, which felt that it was indelicate to talk about facts, and so turned to the spiritual. time was divided into periods, and a zeitgeist had to be found for each of them. if one looks into the past it might perhaps be possible to identify something like a spiritual community of all forms of life in a particular period, but when one comes closer to the present, spiritual perspectives become less and less clear. zeitgeist exists only from a great distance.

but even with a cultural division that is as distinct as the baroque it is difficult, if one looks more closely, to discover the common factors. the spiritual perspective of the period, put together by art historians, collapses.

the steam engine is a product of the baroque. how so? well, it was invented by james watt in 1765, at the same time as dominikus zimmermann and balthasar neumann were building their famous baroque churches. the calculator was invented in the baroque period, and the mechanical loom, but also tools of modern technology like the drill and the circular saw. the first flying bodies, balloons and hang gliders were built. johann sebastian bach, the mathematician among musicians, was creating anything but reflections of curved façades or pompous pilasters, not music of mystical edification.

what was the baroque zeitgeist? in one case it was the prestigious appearance of the absolutist state, a demonstration of power unleashed in a frenzy of building. in another case it was the cultural revolution of the counterreformation. building-obsessed italy used domes and vaults, cornices and capitals, columns and architraves, stucco and plaster, pink and sky-blue to show the protestant north its medieval boundaries.

what was baroque? newton's mechanics of the heavens, the cosmic clockwork of circular movements in which the earth is also included, or the enraptured look into the heaven of church saints with folded hands and flowing robes?

the state needs palace façades, architectural shows like military formations. the church had open sky painted in the vaults to make the faithful even more humble, kneeling before the authority of both the church and its control by the grace of god.

in the midst of this cultural muzzling the industrial revolution took place. in 1690 papin invented a steam-driven pump, newcomen built a steam engine that still ran very slowly, and that was as early as 1711, before watt built the fast-running one. in 1760 the lathe was invented, and shortly before that a planing machine with linear and rotating movement, now driven by an engine.

submarines were built, and paddle steamers. and with the development of rivets and screws iron parts became elements of large structures. the first iron bridges were built, the one over the severn in coalbrookdale dates from 1775-79. the first cast-iron stanchion appeared about 1780. soon iron was being used for greenhouses in botanical gardens.

let us forget the notion of zeitgeist. at least it cannot be found at this period, which seems to be the one with the most likelihood of a common spirit. or does something like rousseau's "contrat social" go with the wies church, both of which originate from the same time? voltaire was celebrating reason and enlightened monarchy, rousseau on the other hand was criticizing the arrogance of reason, wanted to return to the virtue of naturalness and founded the polity of the radical republican.

no, times are too complicated to be suitable for a unified theory. putting everything together turned out to be waffle. art history wanted to be a science as well, and scientific probity was demonstrated in unified theories, generalizations, whether they fitted or not.

in the baroque a colossal culture was built up, the world was given a new appearance and at the same time an old world was hollowed out, pulled down. the modern world was laid out.

here we are talking about a third modernism.

this should not be seen as definition of a zeitgeist nor as an historical classification, even if temporal classifications may be appropriate. it is a matter of describing adjustments, attitudes. modernism is too complex for us to be able to appropriate it without differentiation. even the presentation of three positions can only be an approximation. in any case it cannot be understood as zeitgeist.

1

modernism did not make its first appearance in individual aspects, but as a total phenomenon, in the mid

joseph paxton,
crystal palace,
london, 1851.

isambard kingdom
brunel, matthew
digby wyatt and
owen jones, pad-
dington station,
london, 1854.

august von voit,
glass palace,
munich, 1854.

nine-teenth century, in the form of the crystal palace in london, the halls for the great exhibition, the first world fair. joseph paxton had gained experience of cast iron in glasshouses, and now put up the first modular building, using only iron and glass and constructed using the methods of industrial mass production. the building principle determined its appearance. there was no longer a previously conceived notion of form as used by baroque architects. the building principle was the architecture. no art, no decoration were added.

pure iron construction, pure engineers' buildings were not completely new. there had been the market hall by the madeleine in paris, built in 1824, or the hungerford fish market in london in 1835. the first cast-iron factory appeared as early as 1801, a seven-storey spinning mill in salford. it was designed by matthew boulton and james watt. the inventor of the steam engine was involved in building factories in which his machine was installed. the steam engine, only thirty years old, was efficient enough to drive a sevenstorey spinning mill using numerous transmissions. watt also applied his structural knowledge to find an iron structure for an appropriate building.

but the crystal palace was like a beacon. it covered an area four times larger than st. peter's in rome. it was built in six months. all the individual parts were manufactured in series production. the modules tended to be small, and fitted together like a net. the largest pane of glass that it was possible to manufacture at the time was only 1.2 metres long. the delicate articulation made the building look ethereal. there was no adverse criticism. the world was amazed.

the other beacon of the first modern movement was the eiffel tower in paris, built for the world fair of 1889, violently controversial and attacked by the guardians of art and keepers of culture. gustave eiffel was a building engineer who until then had built bold railway viaducts in lattice structures. they demonstrated only themselves, pure structural calculation.

paxton, the architect, later built dreadful neo-gothic villas, and eiffel too was a socially split person, who carried out his profession as an engineer but was at the same time keen to be part of the established cultural world. their works owe their cultural interpretation as structural architecture to a misunderstanding. an engineering structure, whether it be factory, bridge, market hall or exhibition hall was purpose-built for secular events and functions. thus not at all cultural. art and culture lived in the realms of the spirit. it was not until this diversion that a new architecture could be born. an architecture that is as it is, to which nothing was added. this architecture was allowed to be pure structure, pure method.

there were numerous iron structures between the crystal palace and the eiffel tower that have gone down in architectural history as outstanding works. the same world fair for which the eiffel tower was built has the galerie des machines with a span of 115 m, built by ferdinand dutert and victor contamin. the machine hall for the 1878 world fair, eleven years earlier, had a span of only 35 m. admittedly the english built st. pancras station in 1868 with a span of 73 m. henri labrouste built the saint-genevieve library in paris largely in glass and iron, and gustave eiffel and louis-charles boileau built a department store with a gigantic glass roof. in the mean time all these buildings have been thoroughly appreciated and are part of our cultural awareness.

architectural development in the broad sphere of railway building, platforms, stations, sheds and bridges was less appreciated. factory building development, workshops, halls right down to ironworks was hardly appreciated at all. if one takes all this into consideration, then it turns out to be bold to place the start of modern architecture as late as 1911, when walter gropius built the fagus factory in alfeld. why not start with albert kahn and ernest l. ransome's buildings in that case? or even with godfrey greene's boat store, which was built in 1860 but could be an egon eiermann building dating from 1960.

let us place the beginning of a second modern period in 1911. a year before the first abstract picture was painted, by kandinsky. it was said that new ground had been broken. in the same year behrens built his machine hall for AEG in berlin.

in the mean time, expert opinion is that modern architecture started with peter behrens and walter gropius.

but there had already been a modern movement before this. there is no doubt that peter behrens and walter gropius deserve credit for having introduced the ingenious building principles that were already customary in the profane world of industry, into the educated architecture of the cultural and artistic world. even more, they pulled the ground from under the quotation architecture that was customary there. for a time. if behrens and to an even greater extent gropius have found a firm place in architectural history, it is not as the inventors of constructive and functional architecture, but as the architects who infiltrated such architecture, which already existed, into the cultural world of academic building, made it acceptable to the cultural and artistic business.

this first modern movement had already formed all the elements of the second modern movement, which began shortly after 1900 with factory buildings in detroit and highland park by albert kahn, peter behrens' AEG turbine hall in berlin and the fagus works in alfeld by walter gropius and adolf meyer. it is difficult to invent anything fundamentally new. this is as true of reinforced concrete building as it is of building with iron and steel.

reinforced concrete was invented in 1849 by josef monier, a gardener who fortified his garden frames and flower tubs with iron bars, thus giving them great tensile strength. it was developed as a building principle at the end of the century, like iron skeleton construction at the beginning of the century, the pioneers were the french engineer françois hennebique, american architect ernest l. ransome, swiss bridge builder robert maillart and french engineer eugène freysinnet. at first a homogeneous building structure emerged, in which stanchions and beams, stanchions and ceilings are run in together. later self-supporting shells were introduced, leading to new vault forms, and which could be adapted to ideal mathematical areas. but even reinforced concrete skeleton building was fully developed long before le corbusier conceived his domino model in 1916, concrete slabs with set-back stanchions, open to extension in any direction, without load-bearing walls. as early as 1908 tony garnier built a reinforced concrete hall for a slaughterhouse, modelled on the 1889 galerie des machines in dimensions and structure.

modernism was established. the form of new technical products, of boilers and motors, of machines and transmissions also helped to liberate architecture from any formal model. pit-head gear, gasholders, refineries, ferries and silos, making the design process independent enough to determine forms just in terms of material, purpose and construction. so why does modernism not start until 1910, or 1911 in the case of architecture.

why is louis sullivan only counted as part of the modern movement by architectural historians, when he built the schlesinger and mayer department store in 1899-1904 in a way that mendelsohn could not have made more modern in the thirties? why is albert kahn's 1906 winchester gun factory in new haven not counted as

modern architecture although it could have been an early
mies? at best they are acknowledged as forerunners. in
the fifties, when i started to be interested in the crystal
palace, i could only find one english book about joseph
paxton. but the shelves were full of books about gropius,
le corbusier, mies van der rohe.

2

19th century engineering buildings, the buildings of the
first modern movement, were built by technicians from a
technical point of view, but the buildings of the second
modern movement were the work of architects. even in
terms of training these are two different worlds. architects grow up in artistic institutions, in academies, in the
école des beaux-arts, in close proximity to sculpture and
painting. engineers grow up surrounded by mechanical
engineering, by material tests, by statics and kinetics. this
is the domain of cause and effect, of effort and effect, of
economy and intelligence. there one is moving in the
realm of aesthetics, which is particularly affected by historical example.

the école des beaux-arts rose to a man against the
eiffel tower, defending the proportions and order of classicism and other historical styles. but the young students
could get nothing from the past. they were looking for a
new style. jugendstil took over from historicism, first in
brussels, capital of the most highly industrialized country
in europe, then in vienna, paris and barcelona. its aims
were simplification, reduction of means and organic classifications and connections. jugendstil discovered the
square, the circle and the triangle as the most elemental
forms and used them as ornaments after orgies of lianas.
in 1899 a book appeared devoted entirely to the square.
the revolt against historicism and neogothicism ate itself
up and finally arrived at geometry in its search for pure
form.

the next art college generation then discovered that
square, circle and triangle are also the most elemental
forms of structure and function in the world of machines.
technology became a model for the new aesthetics, steel
and glass the new material, rotation and translation the
new movement.

but none of the new architects were technicians, they
all saw technolgy as a formal repertoire, as an aesthetic
handicap in terms of the traditional bourgois cultural
instinct, for which form is the first determining cause.
the artist has a form in mind and then makes it material.
the mind comes first. the technician comes from a

completely different direction. he has handicaps, materials, means, purpose, economic framework conditions. from this he determines a form. it emerges from a process of optimization.

the second modern movement was the conquering of technology by art. russian constructivists could not build machines. they were painters, they painted the world of machines. they created towers and steel structures, silos and cranes as products of a new aesthetic perspective. a revolution was unfolding. modernism, which had already been there for a long time, was unfolding a second time, as an aesthetic event, as a language of forms.

methodologically things stayed on the plane of the école des beaux-arts. the world was seen aesthetically, as form. what had changed was the motif. the new object of art is the technical world. and so it was no accident that the second modern movement in architecture began at the time when the first abstract picture was painted.

both kandinsky and mondrian tried to liberate mind and spirit from matter using almost religious terms. they were looking for pure form, pure colour, the conquest of everything material. the primacy of art as pure spirit from which everything derives was established.

there were conflicts. architects close to the workers' movement and who saw architecture more from a social point of view, like for example mart stam, el lissitzky, hannes meyer, pushed economic, structural and functional aspects into the foreground. they followed the working principles of 19th century engineering buildings and rejected the determining role of aesthetics and determination by formal concepts. but they could not assert themselves against the "painters", who like van doesburg, moholy-nagy, le corbusier or malevich spoke for those who had come from the background of art.

mart stam and hannes meyer have been kept under wraps to this day. as opponents of "beautiful architecture" they died rejected and forgotten.

the plane of argument of architecture as well increasingly became that of painting. people no longer talked of span, thrust, movement of forces, of the moment of buckling, sagging, they spoke of spatial transparency, of asymmetry, of displaced surfaces, plasticity, penetration, purity of form, purity of colour, as though talking about a cubist painting. cubism itself explained the aesthetics of elementary geometry from a third side. it understood all the objects it painted, built up as bodies with elementary geometrical forms, of cones, cubes, cylinders,

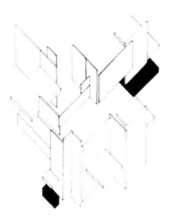

theo van doesburg,
"spatial develop-
ment", 1923.
(haags gemeente-
museum)

adolf loos, haus
moller, wien, 1928.
(photo: gerlach)

piet mondrian,
"composition",
1932. (frans-hals-
museum, haarlem)

le corbusier, maison
la roche, paris, 1923.
(fondation le corbu-
sier, paris)

jacob berend
bakema and gruppe
opbouw, alexander-
polder estate, rotter-
dam, project, 1953.

48

pyramids. in cézanne's painting these primeval bodies were intimated. in the work of picasso and braque they appear more clearly and in le corbusier's painting they are so clearly present that it is only a tiny step to a building consisting only of primeval bodies. ultimately a building is a three-dimensional cubist object.

aesthetic values were given metaphysical foundations. kandinsky said that horizontals were cold and verticals warm. the left-hand half of a picture strives outwards, the right-hand side inwards. right angles incline to red, angles of 60° to yellow. vertical and horizontal lines, said mondrian, are the expression of two opposing forces, and their mutual effect makes life. he said that a picture creates new spiritual reality. Lines, colours and shapes produce pure vitality. he maintains that space axis and time axis meet in the vertical and the horizontal, the picture is an autonomous aesthetic cosmos.

and malevich created unlimited space in his pictures. the objects depicted move weightlessly. time is without limit. art opens up space and time. threedimensional models, so-called architectonas, are used to investigate pure space configurations on the basis of which architects can then produce their buildings. form is beyond function.

the opposite of all these transcendental statements can also be asserted. why can't a horizontal be warm as well? and why can't a vertical be cold? but that isn't crucial, what is significant is that the habit has been formed of using metaphysical language to label and designate forms and colours and aesthetic phenomena. aesthetics had a lofty mode of being that was no longer open to discussion. buildings were not there for some purpose, but they became aesthetic phenomena as a result of the articulation of surfaces, the penetration of space, the transparency of volumes, the dissolution of perspectives and of the viewpoint in favour of a sequence of spaces and surfaces.

it was not unusual for aesthetic demands to be pushed so far that utility values began to suffer. the second modern period in architecture was applied cubism, applied purism and neoplasticism, applied suprematism. the way people sleep, how they work, how they cook, where the children play, how you control ventilation and light, where you can be on your own, all these were trivial things, and a bed in a mies van der rohe space is meaningless as such. it is nothing but an aesthetic object. the way surfaces relate to each other, the way they work from the inside outwards, the way they create

openings and transitions, that was the task of architecture. simultaneity, contemporaneity of wall and opening,
of inside and outside have to be created, transparent
transitions, fluency of space and alternation of large and
small walls as autonomous surfaces that create a field of
tension.

and now the zeitgeist can be mentioned again. the
cultural pattern of bourgeois-aesthetic modernism, of
art-architects and art-designers is idealistic. reality is not
interpreted from affairs and the state of affairs, but on
the basis of superordinated principles, aesthetic
transcendentalism.

there is no doubt that aesthetic phenomena exist.
even 19th century engineers did not deny the existence
of aesthetics, but they did not see it as a superordinate
and determining principle. it had to appear in the thing
itself.

there is no regulated relationship between two equal
units, like two dots, for example. whether they are close
together or further apart, the distance between them
remains without scale, beyond comparison. if a third
point intervenes, three distances are established between
the three points, and these are then placed in a relationship with each other. they are either the same or different. they can be random or ordered in their proportions,
in other words ordered in certain relationships, that is
the beginning of aesthetics. its job is to juxtapose relationships in a certain way, in other words put them into
categories. these can be numerical relationships, categories relating to content, psychological relationships.

this is undisputed. the only question is the status of
aesthetics in design. and here siegfried giedion for
example also postulated for the bauhaus that the artist
should first have his say.

sigfried giedion had been a pupil of heinrich wölfflin,
he had taken the concept of zeitgeist over into the history of art, after it came to correspond with hegel's
weltgeist. wölfflin introduced the key aesthetic terms
classical and archaic, closed and open, unity and diversity as characteristics of form, and saw art not as a
product, but as a statement of its time. giedion, who in
raum, zeit, architektur wrote the standard arthistorical
work of modernism, the second modernism, introduced
the categorical view of things into modern design as
well, and interpreted it in the spirit of conventional art
history. this always takes the view that the artist is the
supreme court of appeal and that form is the supreme
principle. and this is maintained even though the new

50

technology has created a whole range of forms that do not fit in with the classical way of looking at things, like umbrellas, ribbed cylinders, fittings, threaded joints, fans, electric light bulbs, gear transmissions.

is it possible to interpret a factory chimney using the categories of classical art history? is it classical or archaic? is it open or closed?

you can always distinguish zeitgeist. then the chimney points to realms beyond the earth. it strives upwards, exploding space and time. rather less is said about smoke, exhaust gases, soot, polluted air, on the other hand. whereas in kandinsky the vertical, which is warm, meets the horizontal, which is said to be cold. the thing, before it can be a thing, has to radiate world feeling.

if architecture and design are a world statement in this sense, then it will hardly be surprising that their status as a space-time structure is also enhanced by that of history. architecture is conducting a dialogue with architectural history. it is speechless without historical quotation. adolf loos was aware of this when he reactivated the ancient column. post-modernism is a continuation of the modernism that communicated world feeling. cubism itself always used to quote history, and enriched the new language with the set-pieces of tradition. it was bound to happen that historicism would also catch up with modernism. today's design is bauhaus plus palladio. chairs have appeared recently with a mahogany empire back, two legs in pear wood and two in bent steel tubing. the seat is perforated metal.

the new wave has plundered kandinsky's entire formal repertoire. artistic freedom is expressed in design freedom. and an historical quotation always goes well with all the coloured triangles, stripes, circles and segments of circles.

this is certainly not a continuation of historicism. old things are not simply being copied. there are now books like seneca *für die manager*. it goes down well if you can work a classical quotation into a speech about economics. so why shouldn't hotels or office blocks have portals that could be from a pharaoh's tomb or the baths in pompeii?

if design and architecture are given aesthetic motives there is no reason why classical aesthetics should not be included as well. what goes to make the modern zeitgeist is that it breaks down barriers, barriers of space and barriers of time.

the parallel with the eclecticism of the ancients is clear. hadrian had all the art that he saw on his

iakov chernikov,
architectural study,
1932.

hannes meyer and
hans wittwer,
petersschule, basel,
project, 1926.

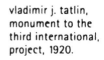

vladimir j. tatlin,
monument to the
third international,
project, 1920.

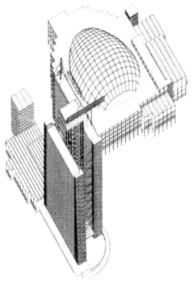

hannes meyer and
hans wittwer,
league of nations palace,
geneva, project, 1927.

campaigns brought together in the park of his tivoli villa, and thus demonstrated the cosmopolitan dimension of his world empire. the result was superficial formalism and boredom. food consisted only of froth.

3

the third modern movement does not yet have a beacon, if we discount the pompidou centre, which is truly exceptional. the third modernism is not aiming to create monuments, because it wants to be objective.

for me there is nevertheless a building that marks the beginning of the movement. it is only a private house, but with the status of the katsura palace in kyoto: it is charles eames' own home. in contrast with the sleeping area in a house by mies van der rohe, the bedroom here is not for aesthetic representation of a bed, it is a room for sleeping in. it is a habitable building, made for use. it was built in 1949, a steel skeleton building using stan- dard industrial elements. the house has the character of a studio. the whole way of life is that of a studio. there is no smart living room, no drawing room, no second liv- ing level. it does not break down into cult and everyday. everyday is the cult. use is what makes the house.

charles eames, by the way. he was modernism's first non-ideological designer. his chairs do not cling to the aesthetic of the tubular steel chair, their outlines derive from their purpose and are not a manifestation of the cult of square, circle and triangle. for eames sitting can- not be forced into a particular geometry. the shells of his chairs and armchairs respect the human body. he would never have entertained the idea of making people sit on chairs with flat boards or cold metal, as is necessary today, for the sake of form.

eames created the chairs and seats of the century, some on castors, adjustable, using materials appropriate to the thing itself. more or less all today's chairs go back to charles eames. first he used moulded shells. he had developed them during the war as leg and arm coverings for wounded soldiers. he sought out minimalized steel structures, professional ones, in other words highly tech- nical connection techniques, had most of the metal parts manufactured as castings after a minimization process, and made possible adaptable profiles that taper down or get wider. his college chair is of the same quality as the manager armchair, that almost moves with the body, bobs about, leans, runs along and is height-adjustable.

do we have any idea what the next model would have looked like if eames had lived longer? we do not. eames had no style, he exerted his intellect in order to find the best way of sitting, what materials are best suited to it and how the whole thing can best be manufaetured, what technology top industry offers us for this today. and there are many answers to this. and there are all the more the more we can emancipate ourselves from notions of form and lock aesthetics out of the room.

for the second modern movement of artists like mies van der rohe or le corbusier the technical repertoire was limited to material in the standard form prescribed for it by industry. eames was a process technologist. he could do nothing with outlines on their own. it was only in the moulding and combination of steel, wood or plastic that technical quality developed. technology is exploited fully only if you are in control of the material's moulding qualities, and the ways in which it can be processed. and then an important part is played by the degree of intelligence with which the various parts can be attached and combined.

probably everbody knows the situation: you walk someone home, you're deep in a serious discussion, then you have to go all the way back again because the discussion isn't over, and so on. i once spent half the night with walter gropius walking between his home and my hotel. it was in boston in the fifties. even then the subject was: does the use of technical materials make something modern architecture? we were trying to evaluate the work of konrad wachsmann. wachsmann and gropius had developed a building system using industrially prefabricated components, and the real problem with this was combining them. wachsmann focused all his attention on this, and developed a fastening that was almost a machine part. gropius resisted this. he said that architecture had its eye on a general concept, it mustn't degenerate into mere metalwork. the only function of technology was to make new materials available. we did not reach an agreement that night.

it sends shivers down my spine when i see profiles as such being cultivated in architecture, and the way in which they are violently welded and combined, all under the compulsion of simplifed form. an incorrect joint causes me physical pain. for me architecture is process technology and application technology, like mechanical engineering. steel profiles are only raw materials.

spoked wheels for bicycles are complex products. the rim with its crosssection designed to accommodate the tyre, the tensible spokes, their layout, the hub, the tube, all this combines to make something absolutely convincing. if the ideology of so-called new building had been followed, a circular disc would have been cut out of a solid material and painted red or yellow or blue. and indeed there are models of this kind by rietveld, where the wheel appears in what is certainly its simplest form, but using prehistoric technology.

real technology is different. it is intelligence made material with the aim of achieving the best solution with a minimum of effort.

in architecture norman foster is a man who thinks similarly to charles eames. his steel structures come from the factory, not from the ironmonger's. they are processed profiles, not extruded ones. the joints are industrial products. rigidity is produced by structure, not by force.

squares and rectangles are not rigid. if enough force is used the joints give. only a diagonal makes it rigid. it divides the rectangular surface into two triangles. and a triangle is always rigid. its shape cannot be distorted. intelligent building is building with triangles.

in the purist architecture of mies van der rohe there are only rectangles. diagonals do not occur. they are not allowed to appear because they would disturb the concept of classical repose: the language of shapes, of rectangular shapes, would be disturbed.

even with norman foster one never knows what the next building will look like. the scope for intelligent solutions is immeasurable, but only if you are in a position to ask questions. a person who cannot ask questions repeats himself.

norman foster has the technical perceptions of an aircraft builder. he knows how to construct a rotor head for a helicopter, which translates the energy of the engine into the movement of two rotating blades that have to have their angles altered while rotating. he has a weakness for aircraft, in the construction of which expenditure of material and energy is minimized while the supreme principle is simultaneous maximization of performance. his buildings are close to being natural products. plants too work on the principle of achieving a great deal of effect with little effort. in this nature is the mistress, and she always does it with intelligence, never with force.

in buildings of this kind there is a new sort of aesthetic. it also appeals to the mind. these buildings can be read, understood. you discover them. what you see is what it is because it is more reasonable than the other way round. you discover ideas, logic, wit. it is not pure mood aesthetics, dull feeling. there is also no zeitgeist expressed here, no world feeling, one sees one of the best possible solutions to a set of questions.

the third modernity draws on the first one. it is constructive, not formal. but it knows that what is technically correct is not necessarily beautiful. technical optimization and visual optimization are two different things, but even if they are governed by different laws and have to be treated according to their own categories they cannot be separated. beauty is dependent upon what is right, and what is right must be developed within the best possible aesthetic framework.

art-beauty as autonomous beauty has no place in technology. on the other hand, what is correct and technically the best also inclines to develop within an aesthetic order. sometimes more beautiful is better.

this complexity, which may have a parallel in psychosomatics, where again there is a mutual dependence of the one and the other, is structured differently in the third modernity from the first one. it is particularly fortunate that today architect and engineer have approached each other. it is exemplary that the london engineering office of ove arup is associated with such important architects as richard rogers, renzo piano, norman foster and michael hopkins, all pioneers of the new conception in architecture. one has the impression that the engineers would like to be architects, and make architecture, while the architects are developing an ambition to move ito the construction industry. both groups, engineers and architects, are getting closer to each other. though everyone knows that no problems are solved by uniting two disciplines. here too nothing but mediocrity will be produced if the design process is not creative and ingenious. there are also buildings where it is clear that architect has relied on engineer and engineer on architect. they show no interplay of minds, no ideas, no ability to think.

today architecture has been reduced to the level of the fashion magazine. periodicals are studied, building methods are no longer learned, at most to the extent that a fashion designer has to know how clothes are sewn together. in the mean time technical building has also become fashionable. the new aesthetics is called high-tech. technology is used only as a piece of scenery, as a pattern catalogue for new design ideas.

art deco could easily have gobbled up the bauhaus. art deco was the official art of the twenties. the bauhaus was unofficial. and sometimes it seems as though high-tech could gobble up the third modernity. many of the things today that look as though an architect had worked with a building engineer are simply cribbed as outward appearance, a new formalistic fashion.

there is no question that the third modernity is descended from constructivism. but constructivists were painters, not technicians. the world of machines, by which they were fascinated, was translated into machine rhetoric, the industrial buildings produced more painterly motifs than structural stimuli. vladimir tatlin's design for a monument for the third internationale, the principle work of constructivism, was only the illusion of a construction, only its aesthetic dream. even naum gabo said to tatlin at the time that he should either build functional buildings and bridges or make pure art, but not both. a convincing structure is always rational and minimalized, never expressionist. there is no such thing as expressionist technology.

to this extent constructivism had more the significance of a manifesto, which gained its weight as a programme, not as an exemplary demonstration.

this programme wants to abolish the division between art and life, between society and individual, between technology and craft, between body and spirit.

everything is design. everything can be created. everything, existence, everyday life, private and public needs, strength, spirit, the responsibility of design, and of creative grip.

as far as significance was concerned, the russian architects' actual buildings lagged behind their programme, which caused a new outbreak of hostilities. hannes meyer versus walter gropius. el lissitzky versus le corbusier, mart stam versus theo van doesberg, vladimir tatlin versus piet mondrian, alexander rodshenko versus lászló moholy-nagy. the revolutionary passion of the twenties was such that "down with art!" could be shouted, and indeed even mondrian doubted whether art, autonomous aesthetics, would still be permissible in future.

if we were concerned with an historical evaluation here there is no question that we would have to point out the great initiatives taken between the weissenhof estate in stuttgart and the neubühl estate in zurich, point out estates by ernst may or j.j.p. oud and achievements like the frankfurt kitchen that were so impressive for their period. however, it is a matter of positions and mentalities. working out the outlines of these means that historical or personal significance sometimes have

57

to take a back seat. thus it is not an evaluating historical judgement if one says of constructivism at the time, which produced a series of important buildings, that it paid less attention to construction than constructive appearance.

new constructivism, the third modernity, as recognizable in the centre pompidou, leaves the notion of structures built of steel sections behind. the buildings become devices, with parts specially shaped for the task in hand. parts of the building that have to withstand pressure look different from those that have to withstand pull. a construction like the centre pompidou is no longer a monolithic structure. it is based on a clearly legible interplay of tensile and pressure forces with very different development of the constructive parts, which join to form a whole with some joints that are very complicated in places. joints take the form of bones, brackets taper according to the stresses to which they are submitted.

some stimulus may have come from archigram. in about 1960 these draughtsmanarchitects needed machine forms for their paper designs of futuristic cities.

but the decisive criterion is a new understanding of structural statics. building takes its orientation from building itself. architect and engineer co-operate. each has his own sphere of authority, but there is no dividing border. each romps around in the other's field.

for a statics expert bridge building is a standard, which tries to reach a maximum with a minimum, to a certain extent, a maximum of stability with a minimum of material and technical effort. the centre pompidou or the hong kong and shanghai bank in hong kong transfer the technology of bridgebuilding to architecture. this creates new spheres of activity for the architect, who is now free to shed the formal constraints of square, circle and triangle, free to fulfil programmes. anyone who is keen on form must develop it, bring it out, let it grow, reveal it, allow it to unfold, before he knows what it looks like.

the virtue of science is transferred to design. the virtue of science is curiosity, not knowledge. a scientist who already knows what he wants to know is already not a scientist any more. a scientist wants to find. he does not apply knowledge. he learns to question and practises finding.

this is also the virtue of the new architect, the new designer. life is increasingly becoming an unknown cosmos. every individual used to know sooner than he does now where his life will lead. the world and time are

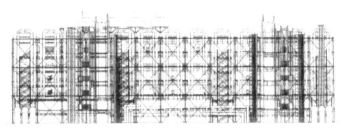

renzo piano and
richard rogers,
centre georges
pompidou, paris,
1977.

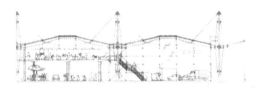

richard rogers,
INMOS factory
building,
newport, 1982.

norman foster,
renault distribution
centre, swindon,
1982.

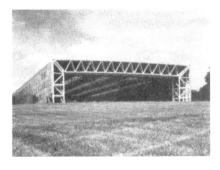

renzo piano, menil
collection museum,
houston, texas,
1986. (photo: paul
hester)

norman foster,
sainsbury centre for
visual arts, norwich,
1978.

59

opening up. we have to grope our way forward into the unknown. the zeitgeist no longer has any answers. we design because we seek, not because we know.

the result will always be different according to procedure people who know incline towards designing body work for cars. they pack things up in their notions. they enclose them. but seekers find open, structural solutions.

form shows its origins. it is a testament to its own evolution. and by doing this it also satisfies the need to be able to read and understand it. it is a kind of record. it would not be satisfied simply with being a mere phenomenon, as is evidently the case with ieoh ming pei's buildings. showing how something is made is obviously a different design culture from simply presenting the result and hiding its origin. the primacy of the bodywork designer has been broken.

it is no longer enough simply to show something. packaging is a lie. everything looks good today. we know what looking good means. especially for people who want to take you for a ride. we need to be able to look through the presentation. the customer is getting curious as well.

today it is design itself that is revealing. not the zeitgeist any more. the design shows what happened, what is germane. the answers no longer lie in the realm of the spirit, even if it is the spirit of the times, they lie in the thing itself. bread itself shows whether you can still eat it, water itself shows whether you can still drink it, the air shows whether you can still breathe it. the zeitgeist is too prone to generalization.

the world is in an alarming state. a quarter of all species of plants and animals are fundamentally threatened or extinct. we treat nature as though it were something at our disposal as we wish, a worthless property. it costs nothing and isn't worth anything either.

man has reached the point where he is threatening to snuff himself out. it's not that man is man's enemy. no one wants to kill anyone else. but probably everyone wants to make money from armament sales, from chemicals that are wrecking the earth, from cars that contaminate the air with their exhausts. nobody wants to give up the blessing of consumer society, which is threatening to suffocate the whole world in excess consumption.

this lunatic split condition can only be tolerated through distractions. the most subtle of these is aestheticization of the world. we are practising giving it new and perfect make-up, and we simply tip the chemical remains that arise in the production of cosmopolitan cosmetics - and that is more than the products that are produced - into our rivers. life is only tolerable if it gets more beautiful. thinking is only tolerable if the head too takes part in the fashion of theories that are new every day, in the post-modern consumption of jaunty postulates. the rubbish that is suffocating us can only be tolerated in new buildings made of glass, brass, marble and chrome. the trees that are getting stunted can only be tolerated through artificial flowers that get ever bigger and more beautiful. the plastics industry has reached such a state of perfection that the eye can no longer tell the difference between nature and the artificial, you have to feel the flowers first.

painting has never been as beautiful, as luxuriant and as grand as it was at the time of makart, when the workers' battles were raging in the factories and streets. never have so many museums been built as today, all in the style of the second modernity, and this at a time when we are threatening life itself.

chairs are to be sat on. man does most of his work sitting down, and recently he has also moved about sitting down. we sit in the car, the aeroplane, the bus, the train. but if someone were to look for a seat for his car at the furniture fair in milan or cologne he wouldn't find one. today's designer is not interested in better sitting, but in the chair, the chair as an object of self-presentation, the chair as creative expression, the chair as a work of art. it is a declaration of cultural bankruptcy that designers can fill entire fairs with their chairs but not produce seats for drivers.

the misunderstanding we labour under today runs like this: what is modern is the use of new materials, we should think in steel, aluminium and glass. but the most beautiful selection of modern materials, with all the modern profiles, all the so-called semi-finished products of technical civilization, cannot produce a single technical object. even railway lines, which really are pure profile, are of no instrinsic value. everything depends on how they are connected, connected with sole plates, connected with other rails, how they are embedded in a level stone embankment.

it is not materials that make the new design. charles eames in particular is a good example of this. he did not use only steel and plastic, but wood, a lot of wood. a technical object is an organized object. it has to be shaped. as a rule the join, the connection is more important than the semi-finished product. the question of how one part is connected to another is the key to a technical structure, to any kind of higher form of organization. the human skeleton is not made up of bones, but of bones and joints and vertebrae. the deformation of the bone defines its optimum quality. the joint, the connection determines its flexibility and thus its ability to operate. i do not know any modern design school that teaches the methodology of combining two profiles. they can be combined rigidly, semi-rigidly, hinged, movable in one dimension, movable in two dimensions, movable in three dimensions, welded, jointed, screwed, glued, riveted or even bound.

an architect of today with aspirations to being a modern architect can scarcely have higher cultural status. his building too consists only of sections, from the bearer structure to the banisters. the connection of a post to a handrail is the result of sawn-off profiles, of

charles eames,
seating.
plywood chair, 1946.
fiberglass chair, 1953.
la fonda chair, 1961.
aluminium group
chair, 1958.
soft pad group chair,
1969.

nobly joined halffinished material. aesthetic fashion helps to mask spiritual poverty, a cult of simplicity is being developed. constructivism or deconstructivism is a montage of half-finished material in simple colour canons of red, yellow and blue, of black and white.

charles eames followed a different principle from gerrit rietveld. for him material was there to be shaped, not to be sawn off, and the central theme of his technique was connection. the rietveld chair consists only of halffinished material, boards and little beams. it is not possible to see how they are connected, nor is it meant to be seen. while any cabinet-maker or carpenter's apprentice in the darkest middle ages would have known that wood can only be joined following form rather than force. all you have to do is cut into the beams a little and push them into each other and they will produce a firm joint, even without nails. but in truth rietveld did not want a chair, but a spatial sculpture based on mondrian's rules. for this reason half-finished material was nailed to half-finished material.

it is almost heroic not to get involved in this sort of nonsense, which continues till today. charles eames is one of these heroes, even though he would reject the attribute, as the other technology, orientated towards construction rather than art is customary everywhere, even in a bicycle factory. it is normal and taken for granted, provided that you remain outside the demands of current design. but furniture is in the domain of culture.

perhaps the crucial influence on eames was that he worked in a factory during the war that shaped plywood into shells intended to immobilize broken limbs. it is easy to shape plywood two-dimensionally, into gutter shapes. by means of skilful incisions eames also managed to shape it in three dimensions. he began to think technologically.

eames' first chairs were made of shaped plywood. the wooden shells then became plastic shells, which led to new series of chairs that have been copied a thousand times, but never equalled.

how do you combine a wooden shell, a plastic shell with a tubular frame to make a chair? you would only arrive at the idea of using flexible rubber if you had the opportunity of rummaging around in factories. his use of cast parts is just as technologically orientated. they are better suited to a run of forces than normal profiles. finally eames even says goodbye to halffinished profiles. the later models consist almost exclusively of specially shaped parts. series manufacture makes this possible. he moves to a different technological standard, leaving behind the approach of someone like marcel breuer with his tubular steel furniture or mies van der rohe with his strip steel. a new aesthetic comes into being. he is no longer interested in a modernism of pure form intended to mask infantile technique. his view of modernism exploded legitimacy of material and pure form, into which the old masters had spun and isolated themselves. eames dedicated himself to ingenious design in which he searched through modern technology to find the best ways of fulfilling ergonomic requirements. and this with highly trained aesthetic susceptibilities.

eames did this casually, and i know this from having met him, he was not an ideologist. he was too curious to let himself be pinned down, even to be pinned down by himself. nothing was too small not to be a sensation for him. he picked everything up, looked at everything, in the background there was always help from industrialists who were his friends, and around him the friends of cultural unrest.

his studio was a little factory in itself. here the distinction between design studio and production was abolished. for his own house, a jewel of modern architecture, he used elements of factory hall construction.

eames is the father of the modern chair. he introduced aluminium casting, height adjustment, tilt springing, the seat shell, the castor. his real achievement was that he was able to show how far technology and industry can be used to press forward to new design concepts. he made the most beautiful chairs, armchairs and rows of seats. but he was not interested in beauty as such, and certainly not that of the artistic fashions of the moment.

hans gugelot

when an engineer designs a technical product, a work-
piece or a memory for a data base, he works in logical
leaps, as in mathematics. he measures and counts, calculates and follows the laws of causality. every effect has a
cause and every cause has an effect. engineers think in a
linear fashion, in a chain of thought.
things are not so easy for designers.
when a painter paints a picture he does not calculate
and measure. logic does not get him very far. he sets the
aesthetic qualities with which he is concerned and
derives them from a target idea. whether the picture is
representational or abstract he is concerned with a
statement aided by an aesthetic quality.
designers cannot take refuge in a rationally analytical
working method that resolves everything into quantities
and makes it quantifiable, nor can they limit themselves
to producing qualities, arrangements of perception, of
colour, of form.
designers' working methods are more complex. but it is
not a bit of this and a bit of that. it certainly includes
calculating and measuring and the manufacture of proportions, but it is more. a designer is a kind of moralist.
he evaluates. his activity consists of evaluation.
there are technical products that are good but an
offence to the eye, there are decorative products that are
unusable, beautiful things that distort the world. there
are products that are allegedly of the highest utility value
but technically wretched. there are beautiful products
that do not convey any more information, that admit no
curiosity, that consist only of disguise.
what do designers have to make? working products?
good-looking products? usable products?
designers fall between two stools. a technically impec-
cable product does not have to be beautiful, a beautiful
product does not have to be usable, and a good-looking
product may perhaps look good only because it hides and
covers everything.
a designer's task is to create order in a conflict-field of
heterogeneous factors, to evaluate.
it is utter nonsense to keep on saying that (good)
form is the inevitable result of function, or that a good
spirit must live in a beautiful body. the opposite is no
less true.
the category of the technical is what is right, not
what is beautiful, and the category of the beautiful is

what is aesthetic, not what is right. the category of information is the true not the beautiful. and the category of use is the useful not the technical.

certainly the product we are looking for is one that functions technically and is formally attractive, durable in use and intelligible in function, meaning and origin. but all these qualities do not evolve from each other as if of their own accord, they are not mutually interdependent, they are not causally linked to each other, and quite often they are in tension and create conflicts.

to this extent the designer's activity is evaluation.

things are not easy for designers. in the last resort they too have to keep an eye on the economic dimension, and certainly cannot work on the assumption that products in conformity with the market are correct, beautiful, true and useful products. junk is just the thing that sells well.

hans gugelot was a dutchman by birth. you could tell. the dutch have developed a sense of pragmatism from being forced to come to terms with the sea, and have an ingenious attitude to the environment. holland never knew the courtly culture of france, and elegance is no more a dutch design category than prestige. the dutch had to contain the sea when it broke through, they had to build ships and canals, exploit the power of the wind for pumps and mills. this developed their common sense, the virtue of tolerance and practical reason. there is a great deal of technical curiosity in hans gugelot's work, but never drama.

hans gugelot grew up in switzerland. here too a type of cultural behaviour has grown up that sees nature not just as a promoter but as a promoter of challenges. just as you cannot come to terms with the sea by virtue of higher orders, dealing with rocks and snow has produced a group approach directed at efficiency, not at great form. the swiss built towns; cathedrals and palaces did not appeal to them. they are interested in a case, not in an ideology, like the dutch as well.

today ideology is written in capital letters in design. american and italian design no longer concern themselves with a thing, but with representation, design is degenerating into sign.

hans gugelot died in 1965. the question is, whether he would have been an upto-date designer today, a designer for american behavioural culture, manifested in showing and showing itself. or would his influence have remained as powerful as it was at that time? unquestionably he was a determining influence upon a whole period. hans gugelot and charles eames, the latter an american who still had the pioneer mentality, were the key designers of that time. but their thought categories were those of craftsmen, technicians, not of manufacturers. their products were not designed for production, but as responses to states of affairs.

perhaps hans gugelot would be especially important today. it is by no means definite that the future belongs to large-scale forms, that market has to determine product and that we shall have to accustom ourselves to a world of representation where nothing stands for itself any more, but simply represents itself.

can there be such a thing as a famous designer?

designers fall between all stools.

there is such a thing as a great painter, a great scientist, a great general. but greatness presupposes limitations, concentration on a narrow field that is not methodologically complex. if a general were to think about the meaning of war, even about peace, his battles would be lost.

designers are like painters who, instead of painting, calculate and measure, they are like engineers looking for proportions instead of constructing, they are like businessmen interested in perfection and usefulness rather than sales, like sculptors looking for structures and technical intelligence rather than form.

even a philosopher who would like to be an educationalist himself as well has little chance of going down in history. anyone who approaches the complexity of life has little prospect of remaining in the memory of humanity like the great simplifiers, the high-flying specialists. Anyone who pushes his mind to the boundaries of rationality or his heart to the most sensitive nerve has prospects of being perceived, but not someone who needs both. simplicity of method is an ingredient of greatness. even an architect must have specialized in either form or technology if he wants to set people talking. This is the real reason for the subordinate role of women in history. they have to think with their hearts and feel with their heads, and thus withdraw from our scheme of cultural evaluation.

rietveld made chairs that look like three-dimensional constructed translations of mondrian's paintings. they were scarcely suitable for sitting on. but they became famous. they were bought as aesthetic objects, as expressions of a style of geometrical elemental forms. only square, circle and triangle were still legitimate, along with the primary colours black, white, red, yellow and blue. they were the expression of a style. chairs were reduced to aesthetic shapes and thus achieved that reduction of simplicity that is as a rule the essence of the fame of a designer.

objects of that kind are then not found in homes, but in museums, hans gugelot made chairs only for homes.

most designers have a style of their own. a rietveld was recognizable as a rietveld. how was one supposed to recognize a gugelot?

what is wrong with a style? we have moved into a world of signs and we very often use objects not as utensils any more, but as signifiers. the things we buy are more often decided by the trademark than utility value. the form of the product, the brand, the appearance are often more of a factor than technology, usefulness and performance of an object, most of which can no longer be evaluated without special analysis under the colourful envelope of appearance.

acquiring a product today is a piece of self-demonstration. it identifies me as someone who identifies himself with a brand. this also reinforces the image function of objects and forces the development of a style that has sign character. how many people have bought braun equipment because they were able to use it to demonstrate their membership of a class of people aware of design?

so what is wrong with style? i am certain that hans gugelot, if he had experienced it, would have objected to the development of a braun house style. with each of his products he was concerned not just with solving a problem, but also with resisting the temptation to style. with every product he fought against the danger that it might produce a style. he had to prove to himself that he was not prone to any style, either to a style as an expression of personality, as handwriting, nor to a style as company image. when he started thinking about cars, and made contact with BMW, he thought neither of building a BMW nor producing a gugelot. at that time it was possible to recognize a pinin farina as a farina, and even today a mercedes still has to look like a mercedes, because the first thing people see in a product is a brand.

hans gugelot was afraid of style and he had to prove to himself that he could resist the temptation to style. he saw style as the first stage in the corruption of design.

every human being is a person, a personality, a figure. but not everyone is a symbolic figure. symbols are not just signs, but identification marks. people look up at them. they are elevations. they permit wish projections, expectations stick fast to them.

design has made itself useful. products are less and less that which they are, they are charged with symbols, carry content and awaken interest that is no longer appropriate to the matter in hand, but intended to arouse desires, and satisfy desires.

a product is always a sign, and part of product quality is that a product signals what it is. alongside technical quality and utility quality, product design also has to produce communication quality, in order to make the product intelligible, comprehensible, lucid as far as origin, manufacture, materials, construction and use are concerned. a really good product shows itself as it is.

but unfortunately this is the exception. today the first duty of a product is not to look like it is, but as it appeals, as it has the strongest effect on market and customers. everything that gleams and glitters has a higher sales value. so pictures have gold frames and cars have chrome strips, cars that look like fish or birds sell better even though their so-called air resistance value, with which wind flow is measured, does not need to be any higher than that of a car you can get into comfortably.

only in a few areas, like those of cameras and radios, has a kind of design come out on top that allows a product to be as it is, that tries to enlarge its product character instead of covering it up with symbol-attitudes.

hans gugelot did a great deal for this as well. until he started designing radios a radio was first and foremost a piece of furniture and had to be integrated into a living room culture that always served show, demonstration.

today a hi-fi set is only acceptable if there is nothing reminiscent of the living room about it at all. but this could be overturned. technical things can become symbols too. there are already cars without chrome, high at the back like formula 1 cars, just to evoke associations with motor-racing. there is such a thing as technical design, but there is also technoid design.

in architecture as well, where almost all building now is prestigious, symbolic, sign-orientated, we experience that alongside historical quotations like the column or the round arch, technology also crops up as quotation, as symbol. any glass structures are decorative and copy technical thinking, instead of developing it. this temptation to make everything symbolic, to make allusions instead of statements, to show settings and packaging instead of states of affairs is the determining trend of modern design.

this is certainly also a consequence of increasing trust in authority. as we experience less and less ourselves, but have everything played to us by the media, as we make less and less ourselves and also do not mend and keep, but tend much more to have everything thrust upon us as throw-away products, we lose trust in ourselves, we do not have confidence in our behaviour, doing and saying, and we worship authorities.

symbol is an authoritarian form of sign. a product laden with symbolism identifies its user as subject, as obsequious.

symbols were once the sign of religious and political rule. today they are usually signs of a supposed cultural superiority. art becomes the arsenal of the significant. anyone who develops the seat of a chair as a triangle raises it into the world of painters and museums, and many people believe that only then it is good to sit on. people are now so devoted to art that it can even be used to sell nonsense and thus ensure increased profits.

but hans gugelot had reservations about engineers as well as about art. like charles eames, gugelot was an engineer-designer. he had a weakness for technology, he wanted to be a design engineer at first. he never looked down on engineers because a designer might have been something better, perhaps thanks to his cultural platform. but technology is something very onedimensional. we once talked about the fatal shortcoming that cars continually get faster, technically more perfect, more cleverly devised, and at the same time their useful dimensions, both for the individual and society, are increasingly wasting away.

this has nothing to do with technophobia. gugelot was almost obsessed by constructions and besotted with process techniques. but he was aware of the culs-de-sac that a scientific and technological civilization forces us into. precisely because he actually was an engineer he saw the limitations of a technology that thinks only technically. the measure of a good car today is horsepower and its speed. everything is sacrificed to this. one does not necessarily need to be opposed to constantly improved engines, by no means insensitive to the experience of speed if one nevertheless sees a car first and foremost as a humane object and therefore evaluates not just technical and commercial efficiency, but simply as an item of practical use as well.

the contemporary alternative wave very often takes on traits hostile to technology. the cult of the hand-made is blossoming again. but hand production can be

hans gugelot and
dieter rams, braun
sk 4 radio and re-
cord player, 1956.

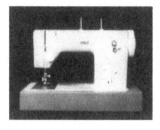

hans gugelot,
herbert lindinger
and helmut müller-
kuhn, pfaff 80 sewing
machine, 1959.

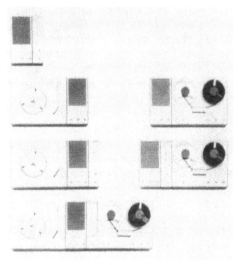

hans gugelot and
herbert lindinger,
hi-fi component
system, study,
1959.

hans gugelot,
kodak carousel S slide
projector, 1963.

72

very hostile to human beings. every farmer is well aware of the advantages of machines.

i hear that some people keep a pebble in their pocket to play with. hans gugelot chose a ball-bearing. two rings sliding resistance-free provide a worthwhile manual experience. but a hand-made ball-bearing is a contradiction in itself. such precise bearings cannot be made by hand.

it is not surprising that he usually started work with technical function models. first of all he questioned every technical solution and used simplified apparatus to check whether performance could be improved. for a long time his carousel for kodak consisted of a slide projector without a casing, so that he could check the technology. he was an introverted technician in all this. his approach was not to shoot at the moon, but to find more intelligent solutions.

hans gugelot was no theoretician. but he was also not a practical man. so what are you if you are not a theoretician and not a practical man either?

he was in command of all his faculties, used his head as few people do. he lived his tasks. what he did was not an occupation, it was his life, and his life was his occupation. this was not a subject working on an object. his persona lived in the way in which he solved a problem. he needed neither the panorama of art, nor the panorama of literature, only music would not let him go. before he came to ulm, in switzerland, he played in a jazz band, and when he was listening to music he occasionally picked up his ukulele and played along. his work also determined his relationship with his fellow men. his friends were also partners in his work.

it can be put down to hans gugelot that he extended utility value as a design category by adding the concept of system. he saw greater utility value in a variable furniture system made up of elements in the sense of self-determination than in an accumulation of cupboards, however beautiful and craftsmanlike they might be. purchasers can put together his own made-tomeasure container systems, according to inclination, interests, requirements and conditions. cupboards, shelves, compartments can be built up in all heights and widths according to opportunity and inclination. a system like this, that establishes freedom, that achieves a greater humane quality, that also of course presupposes creative intelligence and an inclination to manufacture, not just consumers, a system like this can only be produced with the precision that is the hallmark of technical production

methods. industrial manufacturing methods are a prerequisite of utility-value extensions, and also include
the time factor. a system can grow and shrink, be
modified according to life phases. as a system it
remains constant.

one would not be so bold as to assert that our consumer virtues are so developed and our inclination to
self-determination so deeply anchored that the prestige
cupboard is not still the market best-seller. and the
market best-seller in both the fine antiques business
and in the take-away furniture store. nevertheless
design thinking, our demand made on utility value, has
become both more analytical and more methodical and
has left the idyll of home- and handmade things
behind.

the weakness of contemporary design lies in the fact
that it has not succeeded in developing a working catalogue of utilities that goes beyond household empiricism.
this is because technology and economy are measured
not by content and meaning but by sizes. turnover can
be expressed precisely in figures, which leads to the fatal
conclusion that a large turnover is an indication of an
outstanding product.

thus even today design has not been able to free itself
from the misunderstanding that only the beautiful hand-
made product, glass, porcelain, cutlery, fulfils the
demands of humane use. but the converse is also true: a
large turnover is not a contradiction as far as optimum
utility values, good products, are concerned.

as a designer gugelot never had to say goodbye to the
notion that design was the creation of good individual
objects. he started as a designer with a highly flexible
furniture system the quality of which could only be achieved by technical manufacture. with this he also abandoned the doctrine that only natural materials were
good, he used melamine resin boards.

nowadays wall unit systems, kitchen systems, office
equipment systems are taken for granted, but someone had
to make a start and release that programme philosophy
from clutches of beautiful, hand-made, individual pieces.

gugelot saw his system not just as a concrete offer,
he saw a design principle in it that was to prove its
validity in appliance construction as well, and in architecture, and in town planning.

the notion of an end product was no longer sought
after. this end product had evaporated. the result could
look like this or like that, according to requirements. in
the beginning was the element. a few boards, joined

together with standard connections, could be put together as units, a speaker, a shelf. and then the most varied programmes grew from the units.

in methodological terms the relationship of constant to variable, of something standard to the final shape you wanted, of element to programme, was opened up.

it is hardly possible to reproduce today the feeling that moved us when we no longer needed to understand freedom and variability, in the personal and political spheres as well, as the opposite to standards and fixed values, but as something mutually dependent. it is only the accurate element, the strict method that creates openness, allows creativity, makes imagination possible. rational methods and exact elements, exact standards and precise manufacture opened up free space for one's own programmes.

we broke up standardization, which as such led to compulsion, schematization and uniformity. we forced the grid to serve as stimulus. the game emerged from repetition of the scheme. it was precisely by affirming standards that we made a new kind of free play possible. we had a ladder on which we could climb higher than ourselves. we affirmed the laws of technology, in order to open up the realm of unlimited variations.

when i say we it is because i had the same experience in the field of typography as gugelot in the field of product design. what gutenberg did with type, making diversity possible and at the same time greater productivity through splitting down into elements, we also tried to extend to type area and layout, which over the centuries had stiffened into standardized severity. we attempted to conquer the scheme of new typography as well by schematizing the basic elements.

the alphabet has 25 letters, and all the thoughts in the world can be captured by it. taking type back to letters and their standardization rather than to words was the prerequisite for new freedom of the word. we hoped for similar things in the field of design.

at that time we had only concerned ourselves with programmes to a modest extent. system theory as such, the rules of combination and permutation gave us the elated feeling of entering new territory. the methodology of series and series and mass production extended to an open-form design concept. we were naïve enough to see an open society realizing itself from the availability of open systems.

we saw programmes as technical offers. a food processor was to be extended into a kitchen programme, at the end of which it could be that the food processor might disappear. perhaps only a power take-off shaft would be left, and the focus would move from the machine to optimizing kitchen processes like stirring, cutting, mixing, slicing, pressing.

but what was cooked in the kitchen was not yet a question that affected design. so we can overlook the fact that hans gugelot, as a designer, also had his limitations from today's viewpoint. these are linked to his early death. this in a double sense. there is no question that someone as sensitive as hans gugelot would have developed further. his optimistic approach to industry and technology would however have become more sophisticated, if not more sceptical with reference to today's realities.

but it was precisely then that people started to ask: what is the whole thing for? where does the availability of open systems take us? what does industry make of our design ranges? what does society do with a neutral design? we began to grasp the problem of problems. we began to have doubts in the belief that making open systems available involved open application.

i do not exclude the possibility that given the intensity with which hans gugelot was a designer, his death is linked with the conflicts that were in the air and also already starting to show themselves, to the extent of arguments with his friends as well.

designers are moralists. their life is not easy. instead of following natural laws, fathoming them and applying them technically, they fall between all stools. they have to choose and decide between diverse factors and find a credible resultant. they never know what is going to emerge if they have not already succumbed to a style. they have to resolve tensions, differences and conflicts arising from the various demands made on a product. ultimately they even have to ask themselves something that a technician asks least of all, and a businessman even less, and that is, what the product is supposed to be for. who could put up with that?

flying machines by paul mc cready

presumably everyone flies in their dreams some time. usually difficulties arise immediately with the feeling of really flying. is there enough energy, enough balance, will i crash?

flying is not just a dream for mankind, flying is nature's dream, a dream of life itself. the development of living things begins in water. water supports and brings security. but life has developed mechanisms for coming on to dry land, and a desire to fly imbues our dreams as well. life has made countless attempts to raise itself into the skies. successfully. this certainly gave wings to men's dreams as well.

in our century man has also managed to raise himself into the skies, not by his own physical strength, but with the help of flying machines, first driven by engines, but now with the aid of his muscle power.

there was no reason to assume that the americans would be the first to build an aeroplane driven by muscle power alone. certainly the wright brothers from dayton, ohio, were the first to develop the technique of flying, lindbergh was the first to fly the atlantic solo. but before that the germans made the world sit up.

the treaty of versailles forbade the germans to build up an air force. for the first six months after signature it was even forbidden to build aircraft and aero engines. existing stocks were destroyed. this brought about an enormous development of gliders and also a very early concern with musclepowered flight.

in 1920 a glider flight of 1831 metres in 2 minutes and 23 seconds was still a world record. in 1925 the first german prize for a muscle-powered aircraft was offered, 4,000 reichsmarks for the first man to fly 100 m by his own efforts. 20 m was achieved. in 1933 the frankfurter polytechnische gesellschaft offered 5,000 reichmarks for the first man to fly a distance of 500 m. two engineers from the junkers factory in dessau, helmut haessler and franz villinger, built an aircraft in which they travelled a distance of 235 m in 24 seconds at frankfurt's rebstock airport in 1935. this meant that they were still a long way away from the prize offered. but muscle-powered flight had suddenly become a matter of general interest. despite the fact that the two had not reached the pre-scribed 500 m they received a sum of 3,000 RM. hermann göring, the air marshall, raised the prize to 10,000 RM, though now for 1,000 m, to give another boost to the building of muscle-powered aircraft. a muscle-power institute was even founded, in order to create the scientific requirements for muscle-powered flight and to evaluate tests, including those for the performance of pilots. then in 1936 an improved version of haessler and villinger's aircraft with a new pilot, a racing cyclist called hoffmann, achieved a distance of 427 m in Hamburg, and finally in meiningen the record flight of 712 m. but this was the limit of what was then possible. additionally a german scientist calculated that it must be impossible according to the laws of nature to fly using one's own energy in a machine that was heavier than air, just as there would never be perpetual motion. this meant that for the germans - they believed in science - the game was up. the italians, the french, the english, the japanese and the americans remained in contention. hundreds of flying models were built, by amateurs, students of aeronautics, engineers, in order to be able to rise into the air by one's own efforts. the italians established a new record of over a kilometre before the war.

in 1959 the attempt to fly in muscle-powered aircraft was given another boost. the english entrepreneur henry kremer, who had a friend who was an engineer, and who also designed muscle-powered aircraft, offered a prize of 5,000 pounds. the rules were: the flying machine must be heavier than air and driven and steered by its pilot, it must rise from the ground by unaided human effort, it must fly a figure of eight between two points not less than half a mile apart, and it must fly at a height constantly above 3 metres.

the prize was later increased to 10,000 pounds, and the distance rose to 1,071 m by 1972. finally henry kremer raised the prize to 50,000 pounds, to make it more attractive. in 1977 the japanese held a world record of two kilometres. later henry kremer offered another prize of 100,000 pounds for crossing the channel in a muscle-powered aircraft.

both prizes were won by paul mc cready, an american from pasadena near los angeles, an aeronautical engineer with academic qualifications and a glider pilot who had won both national championships and the world championship. he achieved both successes at the first go with his superlight aircraft weighing only 25 kg, with a wingspan of 29 m, more than the wing span of a DC 9. "ten years before this success would not have been possible", said paul mc cready. the aircraft consists almost entirely of man-made materials like foam, transparent film, plastic tubes and sticky tape. aluminium and plywood would have been too heavy. even the drive chain is a plastic product with a wire reinforcement. only the pedal wheel is made of metal.

the shape is unusual. the stabilization and steering wing is at the front, the propellor behind. first paul mc cready thought that his aircraft would have to look like a hang glider, those super-light kites made up only of fabric and tubes. they had been developed in california, and paul mc cready himself flew them and extended his flying experience beyond gliders. but the final result was the sum of countless practical experiences. an aircraft came into being that looked fundamentally different from mc cready's original intention. the aircraft, braced by many thin wire strings, was additionally so flexible within itself that it was easy to achieve variations, even by altering the wires. this made it possible to allow for the fact that an aircraft is a different shape in the air or on the ground or on a drawn plan.

paul mc cready had made a careful study of german aircraft of the thirties. he knew them all, and used his friendship with glider pilot wolfgang klemperer, an early bird among glider pilots, in order to glean more precise information. klemperer lived in los angeles and was considered to be an experienced man by the aircraft industry.

the first aircraft had a skin only on the top side of the wing. test flights were unsatisfactory. a world record was achieved and retained with a closed wing. thus over 300 test flights were flown until on 23 august 1977 "gossamer condor" was able to fly the prescribed figure of eight with a flight of over two kilometres. the kremer distance record prize was won. the pilot was a racing cyclist. he had had to undergo a rigorous preparatory training programme.

the rules for the kremer prize channel crossing laid down that the flight had to take place without the assistance of motors or gas, that the aircraft was to be driven by the pilot alone, that no part of the aircraft could be thrown out on the way, and the flight had to be from a chosen point in england to a chosen point on the coast of france. the aircraft was permitted to exceed a height of 50 m for a short period only, to prevent the pilot trying for a gliding effect.

the cross-channel flight took place on 26 june 1979, seventy years after louis blériot flew across the channel in an aircraft for the first time, with a 25 hp engine, in order to win a thousand pound prize offered by the lon- don *daily mail*. significantly, building of the supersonic

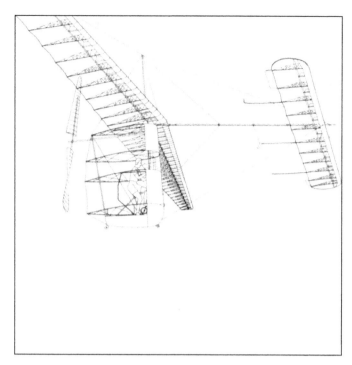

paul mc cready,
"gossamer condor",
first muscle-driven
aeroplane, pasadena,
1977.

aircraft "concorde" as the fastest passenger aircraft in the world was abandoned in the same year, 1979.

with the prize for the channel flight mc cready built a third, improved aircraft that was, however, similar to the "condor", with the same dimensions and weight. the wings had constant depth, and tapered only near to the rump, not at the tip. thus the surface was smaller than in the case of "condor". otherwise all the parts with the exception of the pedal wheel were worked over and made lighter and more robust as permitted by the stage that technology had reached in the mean time.

when the beautiful, fast concorde was introduced everyone saw that a new era of air travel would dawn. it did - but without concorde. there are new parameters for the ideal aircraft now. if there had not been an oil crisis, concorde would probably still be flying today. at that time there was enough energy, and it was cheap. all raw materials were available without restriction, and politicians were saying yes, even to performance maximization. large-scale technology knew no bounds and remained faithful to the principle of previous technical development that every product would be surpassed by one that was even bigger and faster. technology was an unrestricted process of progressive development in a single direction.

but it met a restriction. suddenly funds for constant further development became limited. the importance of performance was relativized. new criteria were applied to the relationship between performance and expenditure. energy is scarce, and funds are limited as well. a single project can suddenly indicate the financial limitations of the economy.

technical innovation is shifting from increasing performance to minimizing expenditure. and because to that extent less is more, the most beautiful and fastest aircraft, concorde, had to be withdrawn from service.

mc cready's flights are world records for minimization, taking reduction of material and effort as far as possible. in 1981, two years after crossing the channel in his muscle-powered aircraft, his solar cell aircraft flew across the straits of dover without any energy from the earth, driven only by the rays of the sun. this certainly does not imply that some time there will be air traffic without oil. it is much more a signal of changed thinking in technology.

when "more, bigger, faster", words that made the history of technology for a century and became its philosophy of life, particularly in america, start to come up against boundaries, technology begins to change over to innovations in the field of reduction and cost efficiency. this is by no means a path of renunciation. it is a question of a new optimum, relating cost to performance, input to output. up to now we have neglected cost culture.

"our entire philosophy", says mc cready, "was that you can achieve a great deal with less." he takes the excess thinking of his country, its political leaders and its economy severely to task, and now that his aircraft stage is past he wants to dedicate himself more to the problem of how thinking can be changed.

the fact that a great deal can be achieved with less also hits the mark in terms of the way the working team that built the aircraft was organized. mc cready is an entrepreneur himself, and director of a firm concerned with mastery of the air as an environmental factor, paul mc cready aero environment inc. but he is certain that the aircraft industry would never have been in a position to build his aircraft. in fact many aircraft companies had tried to develop muscle-power aircraft. experts and large teams, heavily funded, supported by technical aids, were at work. none was successful. they built aircraft as they had always been built, and using industrial methods that shy away from anything completely new. there is less passion in industry. the bigger the company, the more obstinate it will become. even computerization cannot get rid of saurian ponderousness. mc cready's team consisted of workers who wanted to do exactly what they were doing. they were not just doing a job. set-backs occasionally led to psychological frustration, but they learned that mistakes have the advantage of revealing weak points. this was to be taken literally. if the plane crashed on test flights, they learned to see this as revealing, rather than damaging. the parts that had not broken were obviously too heavy for a superlight aircraft.

if light enough tubes did not exist, they were invented, along with a machine to make them. aluminium tubes were too heavy, plastic tubes too flexible. and so thin-walled plastic tubes were wrapped with adhesive foil on a wrapping machine, thus producing rigid tubes lighter than bamboo. many people are annoyed if they cannot open things packed in plastic film as quickly as they can paper. this irritation can be made into a virtue and stability achieved from a material that is extremely light, but tear-resistant. mc cready selected a structural form that was not similar to a glider, but based on tubes and brace wires, as in hang gliders or the wright brothers'

82

flying models. in contrast with a solid-body aircraft, which looks like a bird, he built a bar and wire structure that does not exist in nature.

paul mc cready frankly admitted that he would not have built the aircraft if it had not been for the kremer prizes. here he certainly meant the sum of money involved, but also the fact that there were clear rules, conditions for the game without which the competition would not have been possible. if thirty people chase after a football, that is not a game of football. only rules permit comparisons, and thus a competition. clearly defined limitations allow unambiguous solutions.

the aircraft were not there in the first place to develop new techniques or even new economic advantages. they had been built to take part in a game, a competition.

development of a solar-cell aircraft, with which paul mc cready achieved another channel crossing first, was different. the flight was in july 1980 from an airfield in the north-east of paris across the pas de calais to an airfield in north-east london, a distance of about 300 km. on this day the aircraft could easily have flown twice as far.

there had been previous solar-powered aircraft. robert boucher, an american, made a flight with solar cells in 1975. günter rochelt, an industrial designer from munich, made the first flight in the federal republic on 12 dec. 1980. but his plane, designed like a traditional glider, weighed 120 kg, while mc cready, with his completely new conception, independent of earlier types, achieved a weight of 100 kg, and thus a performance to weight ratio that made it possible to entertain a channel crossing. the solar cells, which were mounted on the wings and drove an electric motor, accounted for 25 kg.

the channel is an historical test run for flyers and swimmers, like the distance from marathon to athens for athletes. but here was no prize beckoning, with the exception of that of being first. at the same time mc cready was concerned to prove that solar energy is a technically feasible and economically viable energy source for all regions of the earth that have a lot of sunshine. this is predominantly the belt of the poor countries of the third world, who need water pumps and miniature power stations.

paul mc cready's successes led him to believe that all today's technical problems will be solved in 50 to 60 years. consequently he is interested in the problems that lie in store for us after those. and here he is less optimistic. successes achieved by technical intelligence in the two centuries since the invention of the steam engine have been overwhelming, but in his view political reason and cultural control among human beings living together are prehistoric to the same degree. this is the reason for his turning over a completely new page in the development of his interests and concerns.

bauhaus and ulm

when walter gropius made us the offer of calling the hochschule für gestaltung "bauhaus ulm", we refused.

i am almost surprised by that myself today. in our contemporary civilization, in which packaging often means more than content, lateral connections, designations and relationships carry greater weight. but someone who had just come back from the war and was trying to build up a new school was in a different environment. so little substance had remained, either materially or politically or culturally, that thinking in terms of relationships, borrowings or interplay made little sense.

of course we were aware at the time of the cultural and political aura that a school would gain from being called "bauhaus ulm". but "esteem" was something of a negative word. we wanted to do what was right, without speculating about public effect and recognition.

it was not our intention to make a second bauhaus, we wanted to distance ourselves from it, consciously.

when i say "we" i need to make distinctions. max bill thought quite differently about this from walter zeischegg, tomás maldonado, hans gugelot or me. max bill did not want repetition either, but he did want a kind of new bauhaus, he imagined that there would be artists' studios for painters and sculptors as there were at the bauhaus, workshops for goldsmiths or silversmiths. for walter zeischegg and me this was unthinkable. (tomás maldonado and hans gugelot came later, but also shared our point of view.)

walter zeischegg and i had both been active in the field of art at first, but had soon left the academies, he vienna and i munich. principles lay behind this break.

we came home from the war and were now supposed to work on aesthetics for aesthetics sake at the academy. that was no longer any good. anyone who had ears to hear and eyes to see had to recognize that art was a flight from the diverse tasks, affecting culture as well, that arose when nazi rule lay shattered.

we had to ask ourselves whether culture and art did not expose themselves if they ignored the real human problems of a post-war period. was art not overall an alibi for leaving reality to those people who were in control of it? was not art a bourgeois sunday attitude of obfuscation so that greater control could be taken of everyday matters? were not the people who were interested in control those who had done most for art?

at the time i was not able to answer this conclusively, but our interests had been completely reversed. we were interested in designing daily life and the human environment, in industrial products and social behaviour. we were no longer prepared to accept that creativity should be classified by objects. would the peak of human creativity continue to be pure aesthetics without a specific purpose, while practical matters and things for daily use were of second-class significance? on the principle that the spiritual is superior to the physical? dualism of this kind is outdated today as far as psychology, medicine or philosophy are concerned. but a poet's word is still worth more to us than a journalist's, and the aesthetics of museum objects likewise more than that of the street. we still divide ourselves into spirit and matter, and need art to vouch for this.

in my opinion what we needed to do was not to enrich art by the addition of a few more works, but to show that culture today must have the whole of life as its subject. yes, we even believed that we had recognized a trick in traditional culture of distracting from those everyday things and aspects of daily life that were prone to commerce and exploitation. art is written in capital letters by people who earn money from trash. eternal values are trumpeted by those who do not want to be caught out at their dirty business. we did not want to be part of this idealism. culture should turn to reality.

we discovered the bauhaus, constructivism, de stijl and found what we were looking for in malevich, tatlin and moholy-nagy.

shaping the everyday, the really real, design had become the platform of all kinds of humane creativity. and if someone was working with squares, triangles and circles, with colours and lines, then these were sensible aesthetic experiments, and nothing loftier than that. on the contrary, it was intended to prove its value by coming to terms with reality, however brokendown, dirty and desolate that may be.

max bill was a bauhaus survivor, and had partially rescued in the schweizer werkbund things that had been forbidden and eradicated in germany and austria. for us he was the authentic bauhaus that at first we could only get to know from books. but bill had another world of experience as well. for him, art remained what it was, while we began to see it as something endangering design. design should develop its results from the object. the danger lay in design becoming an applied art and borrowing its solutions from art.

charles eames' chairs had just become familiar, convincing models for the unity of technology, functionality and aesthetics. this was design on the basis of the task set, design without formal borrowings from art. conversely, rietveld's constructivist chairs were unmasked as mondrians to sit on, unsuitable art objects with the handicap of trying to be useful.

for plato and even for aristotle the material concealed the spiritual. the world would be ideal if there was no matter. the spirit would be free if there was no body. love would be great if there was no sexuality. this view, from which bourgeois society derived its culture business, was generally shared; at that time almost no-one opposed it. the most likely candidate to do so was the dada movement: kitchen stools, lavatory bowls, bicycle wheel rims and broom handles found their way into museums as a provocation.

now all that was valid were statements to the opposite: anyone who has nothing to communicate looks for style, anyone who lives by materialism honours the spirit, anyone who does business is furthering culture.

hugo ball was the first initiator of the dada movement in zurich. but he was also the first to get out of dadaism. rejection of the bourgeois was too little for him. he consistently condemned the bourgeois element in dada and its flight into spirituality. in 1919 he took up an antithetical "philosophy of productive life": "an order of things in which an enormous concern for productivity provides the basis of morality can result from respect for and recognition of our nearest, love of our nearest." hugo ball built up a philosophy of the humane shaping of concrete things, a kind of philosophy of design, against the art of pure spirituality. he developed doubts about kandinsky's decorative curves.

adolf loos also thought that in architecture style and construction were no longer divided like body and soul, and karl kraus no longer allowed language to break down into content and form. form was a form of the propositional content.

at that time in ulm we had to get back to the matter in hand, to things, to products, to the street, to the everyday, to people. we had to turn round. it was not for example a question of extending art to the everyday, to application. it was a matter of counter-art, civilization work, civilization culture.

we discovered architecture in particular in factory building, form in the construction of machines, and shape in the way in which tools were made.

i got to know walter zeischegg when he was visiting a handle research institution near ulm from which he wanted to use material for an exhibition called "hand and handle" in vienna. i made posters myself. my principles were only confirmed when shortly after leaving the academy one of my posters was hung next to a picture by paul klee in the museum of modern art. i was creating for the street what others were creating for the museum. as i signed none of my work, the poster in new york was labelled "artist unknown". that suited me as well. while others were looking for a name and presenting themselves in the market place of appearances, i was happy to be anonymous. craftsmen, constructors and engineers do not sign.

the bauhaus had gone through various internal mutations, internal revolts, like the change from craft design to industrial design, from painting by people like hölzel and itten to that of someone like van doesburg, from a werkbund ideology to a de stijl ideology. it never managed the leap away from art.

on the contrary. the true princes were the princes of painting. kandinsky, klee, feininger and schlemmer. and as ever they were concerned with the spiritual. kandinsky's theoretical work is called *das geistige in der kunst* (the spiritual in art).

kandinsky and mondrian were devotees of theosophy, a doctrine of pure spirituality, which aims to overcome materialism by becoming one with the absolute spirit, with god. for both men, painting was a means of access to pure spirit, and the path to non-representationalism was a farewell from the concrete, from the material world.

malevich in russia was looking for pure space, pure surface, pure colour with claims of the kind that were usually addressed only towards icons. the aim was a remote aesthetic of pure form, of squares, triangles and circles, of lines and colour. klee talked about the cosmos, about prehistory and primeval movement. for kandinsky objects became energy tensions and line complexes. in his painting he sought for purely abstract beings as citizens of the abstract empire with equal rights. everybody was looking for spirituality, something beyond reality, beyond the individual.

but does the world as it is not consist solely of the individual, the concrete? is the spiritual, the general, not just a part of man's conceptual world, to make it possible to come to terms with the world in terms of language? even william of ockham, an early forerunner of modern analytical philosophy, would have confirmed that.

but it would not be correct to see the bauhaus just in terms of this spirituality of its painters. there was a tendency to the concrete from the beginning. the first programme demanded a return to craft, a new guild of craftsmen, work from the spirit of the workshop. it demanded unity of the arts in building and explained art as an intensification of craft. the craft diction of this programme is discernible in the last sentence of the first manifesto of 1919: "let us put up . . . the new building of the future . . . that will some day rise to heaven from a million craftsmen's hands as a crystal symbol of the coming of a new faith."

is it possible to make any sense of this sentence if it is intended to express that the craft age had a lofty working ethos? things were made for their own sake. industry that is locked on to profit and a service industry locked on to profit essentially make use of the delusion that presentation is more important than the thing presented.

architect walter gropius kept the bauhaus open for secular things as well, for buildings, tables, chairs and furniture, however not as such, but as elements of a new faith. the painters found this faith in elementary geometry, in squares, triangles and circles and the primary colours red, yellow, blue, black and white.

that set the programme for the conflict: is design an applied art, does it therefore appear in the elements square, triangle and circle, or is it a discipline that draws its criteria from the task it is set, from use, manufacture and technology? is the world the individual and the concrete, or is it the general and abstract? the bauhaus did not resolve this conflict, could not resolve this conflict as long as the taboo was not removed from the concept of art, as long as it remained trapped within an uncritical platonism of pure forms as world principles.

certainly individual opposing voices were raised. younger men like josef albers, mart stam, hannes meyer and marcel breuer in particular objected to subordination to an ideal aesthetic. they saw the results of their work as products of their working methods, qualities of materials, technology and organization. as empiricists, they were opposed to the idealists of pure form. hannes meyer had to leave the bauhaus. he risked making the statement that art is composition and therefore inexpedient. he said life was nonartistic, that aesthetics was a result of economics, function, technology and social organization.

for the bauhaus the dominant factor was still a geometrical style derived from art. with this it influenced art
deco more than modern industrial production. the bauhaus was reflected more in museums than modern technology and economics.

geometrical design principles could perhaps still just be
used for furniture and in typography, but even for chairs
such formal handicaps become questionable, and certainly so for cars, engines or appliances. industrial production followed other paths, and it was only designers
like charles eames who showed what it means to develop
products from their purpose, from materials and manufacturing method, from use.

we all had our reasons to make reservations about the
bauhaus known. and also about bill's intention to set up
artists' studios.

neither zeischegg nor i were economists, who would
have seen aesthetics as a waste product of purely technical manufacture. it seemed sensible to us to identify
aesthetic categories like proportions, volumes, juxtaposi-
tions, interpenetrations or contrasts and to address them
experimentally, but not as an end in themselves, and
definitely not as a superordinate, predominant and spiritual discipline, but as a kind of grammar, a syntax of
design. the result of a design had to be appropriate to
the task, its criteria were use and manufacture. aesthetic
experiment was an important thing for us, and the conceptual control of aesthetic processes was additionally as
exciting as it was necessary, but we did not consider
newtonian physics more important than nature itself.

hans gugelot brought a technical and inventive mind
into the development group, and maldonado was a theo-
rist and designer who had dropped out of painting.
gugelot created an ingenious technical basis for product
design training, maldonado organized the academic
structure of the curriculum.

bill seemed to go along with the classification of art
and design for a time. the critical point was whether he
could agree to our view that painting or sculpture were
experimental disciplines for determining colour and volume, thus without superordinate significance.

for gugelot the point of the question was the hierarchy
of engineer and product designer. was the designer above
the technician? gugelot had never been concerned with
art and could make an unbiased decision here.

for bill the technician remained subordinated to the
designer. for gugelot that was a pseudo problem. both,
the designer and the engineer approached a problem

from different angles, one from the point of view of technical efficiency, the other from that of use and appearance. gugelot took engineers so seriously that he could not imagine them as subordinate, just as he expected technicians to take the designer so seriously that he did not appear subordinated either. he no longer saw the world as above and below, but as an association and network of different, equally ranked activities. additionally technology released too many aesthetic qualities for him to have wanted to raise himself above them in principle. for this reason he became a technician himself, in order to be able to enjoy the aesthetic reserves of technology. zeischegg moved in a similar direction, and now read more books about mechancis and kinetics than art. he satisfied his intellectual curiosity more at technical trade fairs than at art shows. at the same time he worked his way into the mathematics of bodies and positions in order to come to terms with the laws of volume and topos. he could not place in hierarchies something that for him was a result of different starting points and angles. maldonado and i were concerned with mathematical logic, ultimately to find out that the answers we received to questions about the world depended on the method we used to formulate the questions. here too a vertical world order collapsed. spirit was a method, but not a substance. we experience world orders as thought orders, as information.

one of the first books i bought for the hfg library was charles morris's sign theory. classification of objects as semantics, syntax and pragmatics also gave us a theoretical basis for defining design criteria and interpreting art as a syntactical craft. this had the kind of meaning for us that sigmund freud had for many people, when he explained the psyche as an organization form of the physical.

i learned once more how dangerous a purely syntactical art of squares, circles and triangles could become if it was not aware that it withdrew from the semantic dimension of information. my posters had got into the formal field of so-called "concrete art", and i had to ask myself whether they still served communication first. christian staub, who was in charge of the teaching of photography, made me aware of the danger in my photos that they could become a formal "artistic" end in themselves, and i should not confuse syntactic exercises with information. where had the message gone?

four years after the school opened, max bill resigned. without him there would not have been a hochschule für gestaltung in ulm. we were looking for his experience at the bauhaus. his views on design seemed to us to point the way forward. but fundamentally he remained fixated on the bauhaus as far as we were concerned. he remained an artist and retained a special status for art.

i found myself unable to relate to bauhaus typography and design in any way that might have useful applications. on the contrary, in the field of typography the commitment to the basic geometrical elements of square, triangle and circle, in the design and evaluation of typefaces for example, was nothing short of disastrous. a clearly legible type does not need a circular o or an a based on an isosceles triangle. geometrical type is a regression into aesthetic formalism. a legible and thus functional type tries to do justice to people's writing and reading habits.

things are similar in photography. the bauhaus did pioneering work in terms of the syntactical aspects of photography. but photography as communication was not very popular. it was all about perspectives, light and shade, contrasts, structures, points of view. photography as a means of communication was developed by other people, the reportage photographers associated with the great illustrated papers. by felix h. mann, stephan laurant, erich salomon, eugene smith, robert capa or henri cartier-bresson. photography by man ray or moholy-nagy was primarily formal aestheticism, an aesthetic and formal end in itself, at best syntactic experience. reality was reproduced as a signal, which certainly was an advantage to the meaning of this photography for advertising and graphics. the fact that these photographs are now dealt as art only underlines this appraisal. their formal claim was in inverse proportion to their communication function.

finally contemporary post-modern design can cite the bauhaus. again, as happened in rietveld's day, furniture is degenerating into cubes, cones, cylinders, and all this in the colour schemes of elemental design. the bauhaus's spherical coffee pots and cylindrical flower tubs are immortal for as long as elementary geometry is sold as art. vide aldo rossi.

it will not be possible to avoid indicating that people have discovered today the extent to which kandinsky can be exploited for commercial purposes. his lines, rods, waves, circles, points, segments of circles, half moons and triangles are consumed today as the latest fashion, since mondrian had become too cold and klee too poetic. kandinsky provided forms for today's visual fashion. even architects' plans exploit his syntactical repertoire. the times are again attached to the lofty and the general. art is in higher favour than answers to a state of affairs, than the result of a case study, than a solution to a situation. art makes us a present of eternity.

this brings us back to the dadaist dispute. they fell into two camps: the aesthetes and the moralists. hugo ball pulled out as a moralist and left the aesthetes to get on with it. marcel duchamp, who was already getting fed up with his expressionist painting, stopped fabricating provocative objects to frighten the middle classes.

the moralists also did not want to evade the accusation that the world is made up of trash, lies and deception. the principle of the modern market was based on profit, and neither factory goods nor chemicals nor the products of the food industry sprang from responsibility towards the product and the matter in hand. the moralists had to leave the aesthetes in the lurch.

and actually this situation has changed very little to the present day. the world has not got very different from what it was. most designers have gone over to the camp of the stylists and aesthetes in order to present products appropriate to the aspect of aesthetic sales promotion. presentation is still everything. pity there isn't an ulm any more.

architecture as a reflection of the state

the title "architecture as a reflection of the state" is
somewhat general and imprecise, but it is intentional.
years ago it could also have been put like this: architecture and society. but society, once the enzyme and soil of
development, no longer exists. the economic and cultural
elements, the general weltanschauung that once made
society into a seething cauldron of interests, impulses
and movements is incapacitated, dead. the state has got
its hand on all these things because it provides for
everyone today, in exchange for being allowed to have its
say and make regulations about everything.

the provider state, promising economic security for
everyone and a secure old age, leads to a society with
the attitude that everything should be provided by the
state, a society with no other interests, if we make an
exception of the isolated counter-movements that do
occur from time to time.

and so i quite deliberately chose the title "architecture
as a reflection of the state".

at the time of the welfare state in the fifties, as
described by marshall and myrdal, there was still the
ethical impetus of equality of opportunity. the middle-
class pronouncement that wealth was a consequence of
personal achievement was distrusted, and inequalities
were seen more as the consequence of fate-determined
conditions like birth, milieu and education. equality of
opportunity was the extension of democratic awareness
to the world of labour and education.

what has actually happened looks quite different.
work as fulfilment of personal inclinations, as a category of appropriating the world and as an unfolding of
sense and value has been replaced by jobs whose quality is expressed in income. as in top management,
where you can change at any time from the shoe business to chemicals or car manufacture, content had
become what you wish it to be in less important activities, and fulfilment of economic demands is everything.
lobbies take all demands to the state, which is now
prepared even in the case of painters and writers to
take every risk upon itself.

the tax burden, once the accursed tithe, was raised
without grumbling to thirty, forty per cent, because nowadays even the apprentice at the start of his career is
entitled to ask what the state will give him in terms of
guarantees for provision for training, sickness, holidays,

unemployment, disability and old age, what subsidies he will receive in addition for eating in the canteen, the journey to work, professional risks, retraining or staff outings.

there is nothing dishonourable in all this, and even the culture of Greece was based on the fact that teaching and training, even theatre visits were financed by the state. and it would become a state well to support higher education over and above professional training as that phase of life in which the individual develops and shapes his world picture, gains breadth, height and width, or remains a torso.

the price our apprentice is prepared to pay for this is that the state is then also permitted to decide what the right thing is for his profession: professional image, working hours, protection and safety conditions, standards, quality. the reverse side of the welfare state is the total authorization state, the supervisor state. our democratic freedoms, which thank goodness we enjoy, and the social safety-net that catches us, are based on the dictatorship of the bureaucracy, total officialization of public life and to a large extent of private life as well.

certainly there are dropouts, contrary trends, but i remember the 1968 student movement, which couldn't wait to hide behind the skirts of the state, the point from which most teachers begin their long march through the institutions, finally resigning themselves to being lifeless civil servants, muzzled by the close-meshed regulations of the ministry of culture. others, like the people from *transatlantik* have withdrawn to the spectators' stands as revolutionary dandies and prepared for the silence of the intelligentsia.

and architects?

i myself, a non-architect, have been allowed to build houses provided they satisfied static requirements and some general points. this was still the case fifteen years ago, and was completely appropriate to the conditions under which utility architecture came into being, whether it was a farmhouse or a craftsman's workshop and home. today architects' professional organizations fix architects' professional image, requirements for their legitimization, but also their procedural methods and approval of their product. they fix which grids are obligatory, what profile a window must have and how a wall should be insulated.

i worked on building sites in my youth and knew most of the building sites in the city. i didn't know any architects working as civil servants, but an enormous number of one- or two-man free private architects' offices. that an architect should be a civil servant was a contradiction in terms. architecture cannot be administrated. creativity means breaking away from social entropy, from the uniform mediocrity that results from every set of regulations.

today almost all architects are civil servants, even my many friends who are architects are essentially servants of the state, with a few exceptions that i could count on the fingers of one hand, and are on the long march through the institutions. in this context i think that it is more than a supposition that le corbusier rejected karl moser's chair at the ETH in zurich because there he would no longer have had the degree of freedom of unregimented design that he felt architecture needed. anyone who accepts the tendency of administration to level down and starts to work within its apparatus is going against the fundamental principle that creativity lies in disturbing the peace of the general and exploding the pressure of levelling down and balance.

there are numerous links between state and architecture. i am very concerned to be the first to point out that today's architects more than ever draw their salaries from the state and even by doing this have created a new dependency between state and architecture. this is certainly not something one talks about, but it is important, certainly in terms of content.

architecture is in a dismal state today. this is true of results as well as theory. the distinguishing feature is lack of orientation.

in berlin james stirling has given evidence of his abandonment of modern architecture, to which he has contributed important buildings, with a government complex in which one section has the ground plan of a church, another that of a castle, another that of a greek columned hall, one that of an amphitheatre and another that of a palace. an office in a church, an office in a castle. that is a reflection of the contemporary state.

and a theoretician like vittorio magnago lampugnani invokes architects like schulze-naumburg, schmitthenner, together with tessenov, as ideals of the appropriateness of building requirements and appearance. the third reich is legitimized.

it is possible to make it easy for oneself and say like gustav peichl that post-modern architecture is dead, which can be confirmed at any time without intellectual risk as it is a fashion. we get fed up with any fashion. but there is more to it than this.

the so-called vanquishing of functionalism is a substantial, by no means a fashionable, statement. it is after all a conclusive consequence for architecture to refuse to look for functions when we live in a society that is no longer able to ask questions about what is sensible. what should i do, what is right, where will this end, where is it leading . . .

these are questions that are no longer asked today. life no longer has to have meaning if it can be successful. even philosophy goes out of its way to avoid the compulsory nature of a calculus or a system of values today, for which the pluralistic panorama of views for intellectualistic communication à la blumenberg is much more suitable. does life have a meaning, philosophy asks, and becomes increasingly sceptical. and so building loses its meaning as well.

why should an architect continue to ask about criteria of function, criteria of utility, structure, manufacture, materials, if building is no longer about determining states of affairs but about setting signs and enriching the diversity of the semantic horizons of education?

the nature of bourgeois existence becomes visible. it does not relate to things, but to success. success is a social criterion, a criterion of recognition and distinction. a success is as great as it is demonstrated to be. for this reason bourgeois architecture is an architecture of façades, of prestige. today it even tends to be an architecture of the set-piece, the scene.

there is a philosophy of post-modernism that is much more substantial than a fashion. it says: as human beings we live in a world of signs anyway, so let us build signs. the contented citizen of the welfare and authorization state does not need to bother about setting off for new shores, pursuing new goals, getting over difficulties and establishing values, he is provided for and his spirit can be satisfied with images, signs, quotations and views.

no, post-modernism is not dead, as some people claim, it is appropriate to the situation.

i shall permit myself a comparison, actually an historical comparison, now that history has become the handbook of design. i do not wish to raise a pedantic finger, i am just trying to make what is happening to us today a little clearer.

i do not think we are all too far away from the situation of the imperium of peace, prosperity and education in the good, the true and the beautiful made manifest in the roman empire. there are many parallels that make it possible to assert that we are experiencing a phase of state culture comparable with the age of hadrian.

things were good for people, there was peace, only the restless border areas meant that a number of armies were needed, the emperor built in every style that he had met on his military campaigns and consolidated a culture of rambling plurality that made it superfluous to have a personal point of view. state citizens enjoyed an extended period of education in accordance with classical obligation that made it unnecessary to look for one's own obligation. general standards were high, noble - and anyone who didn't ask what freedom was could enjoy all the freedoms of the age.

it has to be said here that rome broke the back of greek antiquity by adapting this antiquity as a merely external characteristic. the greeks built temples in places where they felt a god might live, never mind whether it was a hollow between two hills, a grove or an elevation. the romans copied the temple as a signal of worship and placed it at the centre of power, at the end of an approach road, raised above a pyramid of steps. the temple was no longer a building in which a god was present, it was a sign of prestige, a sign of the unity of heaven and state, a sign of celestial power. a state like rome did not need architecture to fulfil a requirement, but for reasons of prestige. the temple became a symbol.

since roman times we have used the syntax of prestige like symmetry, axis, order, geometry of basic forms arranged to shift the tininess of the individual and the sublimity of might into an outline that is open to experience. today we no longer cite vitruvius, but palladio, who performed the same service for baroque absolutism as vitruvius did for the caesars.

contrary to the view of our classical education, this roman state, a perfect administrative state, apparently had only very little inner legitimacy and steadiness, not at all in proportion with architectural representation of god-given statehood.

people felt provided for, but not free, they were not in demand. and a few myths from the east presenting man's own salvation as his own concern, jesus' disciples, fishermen and countryfolk from judaea, were enough to rock this state and bring it down.

today we can read in the works of roman intellectuals like augustine and hieronymus about the effect the simple language of the bible had when set against classical rhetoric with its endlessly repeated and formalistic appeals to great models from the past. quotations were invented in the hellenistie state. people educated themselves by repetition and showed their classical models, and no speech was complete without references to the masters of rhetoric. roman sculptors chiselled copies. emancipation from quotation, emancipation from copies was seen as a release from cultural taboos, and it was roman intellectuals, not strangers, who were the first to perceive this new freedom.

but how a state like this, a super-state like this, can collapse is another matter. in this case we are only interested in the birth of prestige architecture and, i have to add, its rediscovery today. leon krier is still drawing cities as though he were a state architect at the time of the cultivated hadrian.

today classicism is also raising its head like a hydra-headed monster, because our state is a powerful state, no less precise in its administration than ancient rome. never in history has the state chivvied the individual as much as it does today. with its authorities, its forms, its computers, its electronics, its civil servants, its uniformed and non-uniformed police it has the individual more tightly under control than did a nazi local group leader the occupants of his street.

i presume that it will not be particularly productive to attack classicism on the basis that nazi state architecture subscribed to classicism as well. classicism was state architecture whenever the state set the tone of a particular culture. the free imperial cities of the middle ages built in a different way from the rising princes of the renaissance. and the nazis had no choice but to conform to the language of the court architects of centralized power.

i am a man of communication. and from the point of view of communication there are only two kinds of architecture: presentation architecture and representation architecture, a kind that shows what a building is there for and a kind that shows how you can use a building to impress. there is an aesthetic of communication and an aesthetic of expression or showmanship. there is speaking and statuary architecture. a policeman does not argue. he is effective as a result of his stature, his attitude.

you can't tell by looking at a palace where the working, living and sleeping apartments are, the façade as a device intended to impress is so much to the fore that the toilet windows are the same size as those in the drawing rooms. a palace is meant to inspire respect, meant for subjects to drive up to, and it demonstrates power and greatness by demonstrating the luxury of absurdity. the syntax of power, axis, symmetry, juxtaposition, repetition, grading, prominence, excessive dimensions are more important than a proclamation of what is happening in a palace.

a castle too is a demonstration of power. its principal use was for social wars within a community, which have been forgotten by our historians in favour of state wars and state victories. but castles explain themselves. they show, each in its own way, how they have grown up, how they exploit the advantages of the site, how their content is distributed, where the servants live and where the lord, where court is held and where the enemy is expected. whatever style can be made out here, the language of towers, walls, battlements, oriels, chimneys, windows and roofs is more revealing than all the decorations of period taste. this is architecture as articulation.

in the same way a craftsman's house is a speaking house, and so is a farmhouse. if an agricultural estate has a drive, a house with a central axis, with a portal, then that is no longer a statement about agriculture, but about power. this is where the squire lives. and the squire does not argue, he boasts.

and if i see it correctly, the current discussion in architecture, the development of new architectural theories, is dominated by the question: is architecture intelligible communication or symbolic form?

the development of modern semiotics had given a new boost to this incidentally ancient - conflict and also intensified it. umberto eco, who attempted to develop a semiotics of architecture, presents the problem like this:

architecture has two communicative functions. one is denotation, showing the technological and functional characteristics of the building, the other is connotation, showing symbolic meaning. and so he says that gothic rib vaulting shows how in the middle ages vaults were put together from individual caps, but it is also a symbol of religiosity.

my own position as far as this question is concerned is affected by certain experiences.

i had the good fortune to spend part of my youth in a gothic cathedral. not in the interior, but in the roofspace, above the vaults, in the builders' stairs and corridors, in main and side towers. just as other young people grow up in a district, i grew up in the complex structure of a cathedral. the secular and technical access to architecture associated with this very soon began to make me

suspicious about the theory asserted from german
romanticism down to wölfflin that a cathedral was to a
certain extent petrified prayer, a mystical striving
upwards, to the beyond.

i was then able to pursue the demystification of gothic
further with viollet-le-duc, who at the time of historicism
wrote a text book on the building of neogothic cathedrals, and its derivation from structural principles, like
almost all manifestations of gothic. and it is for this reason that i see a fundamentally closer link between notre-
dame in paris and the centre pompidou - in their general
view of architecture - than would have been perceptible
from the usual consideration of styles and characteristics
of style, and i learned what modern architecture is and is
not from medieval architecture, however paradoxical that
may sound.

the interrelation between material, structure and form
in a cathedral became clear to me the moment i had
cleared away the rubble that 19th century art historians
had piled up over gothic. and here i learned something
that i would probably not have got to know to this
extent as a factor in architecture: the influence of the
fabrication method on building.

the pointed arch, people have always said and are still
saying, is a symbol. a symbol of forces striving towards
heaven. in reality it is an invitable shape if an attempt is
being made to build rib vaulting with arches of the same
radius, i.e with stone of the same cut.

a vault segment in a cathedral with a square ground
plan has four arches on the sides of a square and two
arches over the diagonals. the arches over the diagonals
are longer than those over the sides. if they too are
developed as semicircles like the reinforcing arches over
the sides, the arches come out at different heights.
instead of this the diagonal arches are pushed into semicircles and the reinforcing arches at the sides are made
into pointed arches so that the radius of curvature is
equal to that of the diagonal arches. the whole rib vault
then needs only stones of equal curvature. this produces
a rib vault with two semicircular diagonal arches and
four pointed arches above the sides. the vaults can be
manufactured in factory style.

this is what the birth of a style looks like, a manufacturing method is optimized by change of form. but art
historians have even less experience of building than
contemporary architects. consequently form is interpreted
as metaphysics, as an idea. form is not longer the form
in which a thing appears. form carries a higher

meaning, form becomes a symbol. something that is the height of rationality in making becomes supernatural, spiritual and a higher symbol in the eyes of art historians and thus of all who believe in science of their kind. concrete reason and empirical intelligence are replaced by an artistic idea of pure spirituality. stone and material, matter, are robbed of their designations, conditions and content, they are a passive realization mass.

plato interpreted the world in exactly the same way. as the realization of higher ideas, as the application of other-worldly principles of the good, the true and the beautiful in a material, in matter that is unfortunately such that it can only make the noble manifest miserably, grubbily and incompletely. matter is a tragic inevitability.

aristotle, plato's pupil, abolished this dualism and saw spirit and matter as two aspects of one and the same thing. but he was only granted temporary success with this in occidental history.

i must stay with philosophy for a moment. karl popper has perhaps not always done justice to plato, but he proved convincingly that plato's thinking was the result of his political attitude, of his relationship with the state. according to plato the state was an institution for the realization of higher ideas and higher ideals. only a few, the better people, were able to lead it and in a position to find and formulate laws. in his eyes democracy was an evil. the goals of the state were not freedom and the happiness of the individual, on the contrary. the people were given the role of belittling matter, and matter is blind ballast.

popper makes plato into an ideologue of the absolutist state, and the absolutist state became the origin of platonic philosophy. if one wishes to rule some of humanity, it has to be forced into the role of passive matter and the world divided into those who can see and understand ideas and those who are blind to them.

the philosophy of higher ideas turns out to be a reflection of power and a reflection of the absolutist state, up to and including fascism.

from this i derive justification for seeing not only the philosophy of superordinated ideas but also the architecture of superordinated ideas, of preformed ideals, as a reflection of the state.

the state has its counterpart not only in philosophy but also in building, and there is a parallel between philosophy and architecture. both can succumb to a doctrine of the superordinate, of the ideal, true and beautiful, and thus completely lose sight of the concrete and

the real. here we should remember architecture by someone like oswald mathias ungers, and his games with pure
form, with morphology. for ungers architecture is not
coming to terms with states of affairs, but establishing
elementary geometrical aesthetics in the realm of purposes and requirements.

of course neither caesar nor louis XIV, neither the
prussian kings nor hitler were devotees of plato, but
wherever the world is divided into top and bottom, spirit
and matter, symbol and function, then a compulsion culture comes into being. the higher is always legitimately
entitled to rule the lower, and the idea always feels it
legitimate to discriminate against the secular and concrete. seen in this way, it is out of the question that
there should be democratic architecture, architecture
with problems to solve, just as there is a kind of politics
that turns to the actual, instead of realizing superordinate ideas.

let us remain for a moment with gothic, or its
rediscovery and reinterpretation as buildings for the soul
striving for heaven. it is noticeable that in the case of
villard de honnecourt, the only gothic architect to have
left authentic records, there is not a single indication
that gothic was understood symbolically as form striving
towards the heavens.

the rediscovery of gothic by german romanticism
occurred at the same time as a renaissance of plato in
german idealism and a new interpretation of the state as
a national state that - usually with the assistance of the
military - has a higher historical task to perform.

fichte and hegel, the founders of german idealism,
defined the state as an essence higher than the citizen,
and both were convinced that particular world-historical
impulses would go out from the german state. hegel
spoke of a new dawn of german culture which would
take world history further. in fichte the notion occurred
that the nature of germany would heal the world,
because the germans were capable of thinking in ideals,
on higher planes than the trader nations of the west.

schinkel, who lived at the same period, was not only in
a position to provide the state with designs for a new,
decorative, neo-classical acropolis, he drew super-gothic
cathedrals of new inwardness and spiritual uplift: the
empire was rediscovered, and the empire of a thousand
years is mentioned for the first time. the kaiser made
funds available for completing cologne cathedral and the
münster in ulm. town halls in the gothic style sprang
up as well as those that looked like the cathedrals in

worms or speyer. the power state always likes to embrace religion, and alongside the countless neogothic churches of the empire this state of affairs was also immortalized on the belt buckle of the army. "god with us" it said there.

in 18th and 19th century historicism the whole of historical architecture was raised to be a symbol of the new state, and even barracks were built to the syntax of romanesque monasteries. at the same time idealistic, neoplatonic philosophy was concerned with the superordinate, the ideal being.

many people were compelled to experience what that led to. after the discovery of super-history and its various architectures the cry went up for the super-state, for the superman, for the super-race. we got all that, and saw where the particularly great can lead.

hitler, the last founder of empires in the series of state-makers from frederick the great via the wilhelms to bismarck, could do very little with gothic. he kept to early schinkel, to classicism oriented towards rome. in his eyes only the romans were great politicians. today people are less sensitive about going back to historical architecture, even though roman classicism is preferred.

there is a decade in this century that communicated the character of a new century to a particular extent, in which the concept of the twentieth century was born and at the same time filled out in the way that is still understood today as a positive programme, as an overcoming of previous epochs.

and this was the twenties.

at the beginning came revolutions. soldiers came home from the war and forced the kaiser to resign. in leningrad the winter palace was stormed and the tsar deposed. in vienna an emperor had not just been deposed, an entire empire dissolved into individual states.

about ten years later those people came to power who countered these revolutions, just as napoleon turned the french revolution to his purposes and exploited it. in russia stalin came to power and developed communism, in which the state was intended to die out, into a new technocratic authoritarian state. hitler gained his revenge for the abolition of the monarchy as a leadership principle by the rule of the party and his role as führer. in rome a former communist and futurist rose to be the new caesar and duce, and parliament was also dissolved in vienna and the state proclaimed as super-society.

for a decade of this century the hope and faith persisted in a new society reconciled with industrialization, a society of responsibility for oneself, self-determination, breaking the dominance of capitalism and the bayonet. now workers too had general franchise, formerly the right of only the middle classes and the nobility.

then a new monarchy came into being, a new empire of the tsars. new york too was drawn into the whirlpool of change. the ancien regime fell on a black friday in the year 1929, marking an attack of weakness in exploitation somewhat later than on the continent.

in this period, between revolution and the elimination of revolution, a new world was designed.

at that time adolf loos, sigmund freud and ludwig wittgenstein were living in vienna, paul klee, andreas feininger, wassily kandinsky, walter gropius and hannes meyer were working in dessau, near berlin. the first jazz concerts took place in new york. moscow had sergei eisenstein - film had found its pioneer - vladimir maya-kovsky, casimir malevich and vladimir tatlin. in holland theo van doesburg and piet mondrian were painting, le corbusier was creating his first buildings in paris and pablo picasso was still busy demystifying the world view of the bourgeoisie. the conveyor belt in detroit was spreading optimism about mass production and mass consumption. metropolises were emancipating themselves with neon signs, picture palaces, literary cafés and the first great illustrated papers for the sensual perception of a new age.

the new society was seen as a product of planning, of functional rationalism, replacing subjectivist book culture in bourgeois houses. conscience was public, no longer hidden in the factory halls of private entrepreneurs. fashion rejected the constraints of girdles, lace-up shoes, lace-up corsets. greta garbo was the first woman to appear in the street in trousers.

i hardly experienced this periods consciously. i can still remember a few details, like the men shaving off their beards, party meetings in uniform and shorter skirts for women.

i can remember some quite heated discussions. we were allowed to think and argue, there was no need to follow custom, convention and norm any longer. the taboos had been broken.

my actual youth coincided with a period of new state building in a style of order, monumentality and symmetry. every month a new issue of *die kunst und das dritte reich* came out. i grew up up with this magazine as others did with karl may. there was competition after competition, at first only models and plans were published, half cities were altered to make way for new boulevards and city axes, on which ministeries, congress buildings and the temples of national uplift were crowded together, garnished with larger-than-life-size sculptures of naked warriors and torch-bearers.

my life began when the state was rediscovered as an historical commitment. man becomes himself through history. the state makes history, that was the religion of hegel, that was the prussian tradition, which was now being celebrated.

but on this level of self-perception state is nothing abstract or administrative, it has to be visible in its buildings.

at the beginning of the nazi period there was still a national component of the blood and earth ideology that wanted to pit itself against the asphalttechnicism of cultural bolshevism, as it was called, with bieder-meier craft.

one of the spokesmen was paul schmitthenner, and an idol was goethe's garden house in weimar, a piain, two-storey building with a high hipped roof. this contained a good deal of the legacy of the werkbund, always good for opposition to the immoderate and the inhumane. but even schmitthenner went gradually over to the planning of monumental state buildings with the associated aes-thetics, planning that was already looking ahead to the period after the second world war and the temples of victory.

the books of the twenties were burned, eradicated. no books were allowed in from abroad that did not meet with approval. modern art was declared degenerate, committed to the judgement of healthy popular sensibil-ity. in terms of culture and history we lived as in a prison, and what a previous generation had thought and planned no longer existed.

and so it is perhaps scarcely possible to understand what an effect it could make when someone came across the first volumes of le corbusier's work.

a bookseller i was friendly with had them hidden in his cellar. i have never had a book in my hand that was as important for me politically as le corbusier's work. here freedom was not an abstraction. it manifested itself in realizations. what for most germans is only a way of thinking was demonstrated as behaviour here.

our ideal of freedom is of the kind described by schiller in *wilhelm tell*. probably william tell never lived. shooting at an apple as a test of courage and a sign of superiority occurs in many legends, spread all over europe.

and gessler was by no means a representative of a foreign power, the habsburgs' ancestral castle is in switzerland, near brugg. in reality the historically documented uprising of the original cantons was against the increasing demands of the nobility, like the german peasants' war. but at the same time a habsburg had become the german emperor, which thus set up the scheme beloved of german romanticism: freedom is a popular uprising by a few brave men against foreign tyranny. in fact rudolf von habsburg resided in vienna, not in the aargau any more.

this freedom is freedom of a way of thinking. it expresses itself in emotional participation with a community that proclaims its will through great men. for this reason the individual can be absolutely unfree, for example as a result of economic or ideological or cultural compulsions, compensated for by the projection of a freedom in which he participates mentally.

take children in a big city. they live on a main road, the children on the other side are cut off, the back yard is not accessible because of light industry, the neighbours in the building protest if there is too much noise. schools set homework, which doesn't make having to stay at home any more tolerable. the rest is television. here a form of freedom that lies in behaviour is muzzled.

but to a certain extent even the bank clerk can't cross the road any more, he is trapped in a profession in which he has to catch up with heteronomy more than be himself. work becomes a career, and the degree of conformity fits in with salary and upward social mobility. he is a free man as far as what he may do is concerned, he can do and not do what he wants, he can say what he wants, but this only as a possibility, as an ideal reality, but between may and can lies the acid test for the value of political ideals. in reality he conforms completely. he even accepts frustration, visits to the psychoanalyst, in order to obtain the prize of the provider state, social status on the basis of income. he does what is expected of him, at work, in society, at home. the reward is enormous. he builds himself a house, goes on holiday to the carribean, can sell off his car before the paint gets dull and cracks with age. his wife signals eternal youth by turning her face into a cosmetic mask with set, bouffant or waved hair, according to what she is wearing.

the price is freedom, if one understands freedom as self-realization. there are no compulsions for him, but in exchange he has given up decisions about himself, not delegated them, for example, but given them up. he will always wear a tie. his life-space is bureaucracy, the bureaucracy and hierarchy in his firm and social bureaucracy, which controls more surely with amortizations, tax benefits, insurances and a pension for all his old age than with directives. the social safety net is not just under him, so that he doesn't fall, it is above him, in front of him, behind him, beside him, the mechanism of his development is no longer his work, but his prestige, showy demonstration of his status. and how does he show it? by consumption, by prestigious consumption. no-one is forced to buy. everyone is free. but anyone who does not buy withdraws from the mechanism of upward social movement. the freedom that once lay in work, in one's own production, is now realized in consumption, in the consumption of prestige.

a functional concept of freedom that understands freedom as freedom of behaviour is replaced for the citizen of a provider state by a concept of freedom that is content with the statement: every american can become president of the united states.

i know that le corbusier's books were not a manifesto of freedom of a way of thinking, but they were a manifesto for freedom of behaviour, and for that very reason they argued, rather than demonstrating.

it seemed to me at the time that freedom returned to building again. i still think this today, even though i had and have a lot of reservations then and now, especially about his town building and the influence of his painting on building.

for me le corbusier is still the architect of the free ground plan and the free façade as the inevitable expression of a free kind of building. i know that people take advantage of le corbusier today, especially by new york architects, as if he had created a new aesthetic codex, a new style. a fundamental misunderstanding, but also one typical of the way the twentieth century is moving to its end.

admittedly, without the work of a painter like mondrian there would probably not have been a new kind of window division in le corbusier. but it is a misunderstanding to see le corbusier's way of articulating windows as a kind of physical painting. for him there were parts of larger windows, usually the largest, that remain closed. there was a necessity to accommodate a casement window or a sliding window for leaning out of in the window surface, and there was a need for openings simply for the purpose of ventilation and which were best accommodated at the top and bottom in a broad format. a window of this kind, say, a functional window, the window as a service utensil eliminates the former bar articulation and also contradicts the present way of making windows as graphical formalism. the three functions of a window, namely looking through, opening and leaning out and ventilation hardly have any influence on the shape any more today. probably because bourgeois culture distorts and covers up the eye for objective qualities through attention to the aesthetic.

most of le corbusier's buildings are piloti constructions, which makes him free, as for instance with the villa savoye or in the weissenhof estate in stuttgart to choose a completely different ground plan for the first floor from the ground floor and a different one for the second from the first, and to behave in a completely different way in the attic storey from the storey beneath it. accordingly each storey also presents a different picture. in the case of the villa savoye the ground plan shows a drive and garages. the living storey has windows and rooms of a conventional kind and the attic storey is articulated like holiday accommodation. it consists of a sun terrace and small rooms, in order to be able to work and live in seclusion. here buildings, as intelligible as a timetable, have adapted themselves to life as it is today, instead of indulging cultural prestige with a representative middle-class dwelling, additional rooms somewhere, a garage somewhere, possibilities to withdraw somewhere and leisure accommodation somewhere.

people believed that the principle of modernism was asymmetry, and took le corbusier's façades as text-book examples of such asymmetry. but le corbusier' façades are not asymmetrical for the sake of asymmetry, but for the sake of the life that is lived out behind the walls. a bedroom needs different windows from a living-room or a kitchen, and a different picture emerges according to the situation of the rooms. of course le corbusier was not indifferent to whether a window was square or almost square, its functionality was controlled aesthetically, but its architecture offered the surprise that being correct is a prerequisite of beauty.

and a great deal of what is correct today requires the courage to get over taboos. le corbusier for us meant free architecture based on reflection about how people ought to live. away with the constraints of cultural convention, away with the constraints of prestige.

and he even created free rooms. a room is a room, one thinks, where is it supposed to get its freedom from. middle-class accommodation is based on separating rooms. the kitchen shouldn't have anything to do with the living room, work is done there, possibly staff might work here. there was even a men's room to which the men could withdraw to hold conversations about which the women understood nothing. the servants had a different staircase and a different entrance from the ladies and gentlemen.

le corbusier allowed rooms to flow into each other, did not encapsulate corridors and steps in every case, made the kitchen an integral part of the living area, let a high-placed bedroom open into the two-storey living area, created rooms that were variable by the use of screens like those used in old japanese buildings. the accommodation had fluent transitions and its areas were intended to be opened up and closed off. that certainly went beyond the necessity of being able to be on one's own, and showed how to make a house into a free sequence of rooms instead of an accumulation of stereo-typed rooms and space boxes.

i experienced le corbusier against the background of the third reich and its architecture. our heads were being banged against the fact that there is an architecture of the fascist state, to such an extent and so all-pervadingly that le corbusier's books were forbidden by the state. i was committing a punishable offence merely by reading le corbusier. an attack on the classicism of dictatorship was forbidden.

and today?

in just the same way as we have hardly come to terms with the third reich people would most like to let grass grow over the whole business, forget it we have hardly come to terms with the architecture of the third reich.

i consider any politics that places the state higher than the individual is a fundamental evil that will inevitably develop abortively in consequence. in our youth we were beguiled with the pronouncement that common good was more important than private good. public interest is superior to self-interest. that sounded good and was also good to use when it was a case of eliminating the individual.

this maxim came down to us from aristotle. for him as the teacher of alexander the great it was the key to political action and legitimized the hellenistic author-itarian and imperial state.

this pronouncement is wrong. the aim of politics can be only the development of the individual, and that means the development of every individual, even the smallest and the most forgotten. the state exists for the benefit of the individual and not the other way round. the common good is worth as much as its concern about the development of the individual.

this is all seen differently again today. instead of the common good we talk about the fatherland. we who have been used as cannon fodder in the name of the fatherland can no longer get the word past our lips. nevertheless this spiritual yarn is still effective. effective again.

the status of the state is being raised again. freedom and peace are no longer the element in life for which the individual wrestles, but the goods that the state administers and that are awarded for good behaviour.

a few years ago individual, mostly young people had thoughts about peace, a peace that affects them as individuals and that they saw as endangered by excessive armament.

today this peace is converted into a higher state good, and after daily official declarations the citizen has to believe that more armament secures peace. peace is not concrete peace any more, but an empty golden monstrance, a word-husk without content, celebrated for the sole purpose of not allowing any unrest to arise among young people. otherwise armament increases economic growth and means that jobs are created.

and just as the concept of peace has become a symbolic empty formula in the language of the new state, architecture degenerates into a symbolic altar. the new façades of town houses in berlin, hamburg, düsseldorf and munich revert to the gründerjahre under wilhelm II, and demonstrate façades with a geometry that usually belongs only to altars: central axis, side sections, supporting base, crowning conclusion. the entrance becomes a portal, the window a decorative structure, the bars become a graphic net, everything is appearance, symbolic gesture. marble and bronze are no longer building materials, but a gesture of the valuable and sublime.

if i had to go by architecture i would have to say that democracy is in danger. the sublime, the great, the gesture of symmetry have always served the growth of power.

behind the façades there is often glass gallery architecture derived from factory coverings. to this extent the period is without a unified trend, but if the architectural journals are to be believed then symbolic architecture has won. that is credible, for everywhere the state is taking possession of values to which it is not entitled, simply to raise itself. they say that bureaucracy belongs to the devil, but an authorization state cannot do without it. consequently the all too secular has to be symbolically revalued. a bureaucracy that is active for the fatherland deserves appropriate buildings.

anyone who behaves well in a provider state, anyone who assimilates himself into symbolic existence, is provided for as never before in our history. he has to fit himself into harmony and togetherness. he has to accept the life form of higher values and a culture of sublimity and will never have to have the feeling of needing more freedom. this is, as the architecture shows, a beautiful world with historical arches linking us to our past. but that is only one side of the affair.

i recently met a friend of mine who is a photographer who was working on a report on the wall that until recently ran through the former empire and separated freedom from unfreedom. as he made his way along it, he discovered that he was being photographed from the other side. he drew back a bit, went on a rather greater distance away and kept himself somewhat covered. that was how one behaved in the "other germany". suddenly he said to himself, am i a criminal then? what have i done wrong? and he went on quite openly, full of pride about his courage.

a few days later - he is a professional photographer - he was doing a report on a doctors' conference concerned with the medical consequences of a possible nuclear war. wherever he appeared he sensed a somewhat suspicious attitude, frosty looks, until he was asked for which information agency he was taking photographs. they felt they were under observation. a little later again he was taking photographs at a funeral of a senior schoolboy who had been hit by a police bullet without anything having happened to justify this. the other members of his form were taking it in turn to keep vigil by the body, at night as well. an official responsible for the constitutional defence agency (verfassungsschutz) was also present. he took a photograph of each of the pupils taking part in this vigil.

this is the state in which we live.

this has to be covered up with a new gesture, with new architecture. the kind you can see over there on konrad-adenauer-strasse in stuttgart, where a new piece of shoddy social kitsch has come into being, that sugary, historically decorative manifestation of state care. i mean james stirling's museum.

recently what is probably the first set of cutlery with which it is impossible to eat has come on to the market. the knife is pointed like a bayonet. you could stab someone to death with it, but you couldn't use it to push rice on to a fork. the spoon is circular, but so small that it seems that it would work for moving cherry stones around, but not to spoon up soup, unless it was some sort of medicine. the fork is not bent, but straight. you can only stab, not pick up. the handle is as thin as a tuning fork. in fact the tuning fork must be behind the design in general. the spoon spout, the fork points and the dagger triangle have the screws put on them by a structure of this kind. this also means that the cutlery is topheavy enough to fall out of your hand easily.

there isn't a second set of cutlery on the market that is quite as unsuitable as this. humanity is making great strides. but this cutlery is beautiful, people say.

people here means: the priests of high art. in the fifties it was still being drummed into rebellious art historians that the art of this century had to be taken back to the application of circle, triangle and square.

even paul cézanne had split the world of appearance up into cubes, cylinders and pyramids, into circles, triangles and squares or, better, submitted his objects to these basic forms of elementary geometry. then cubism turned things round: its objects had become unimportant, and geometricized structure was in the foreground. then it was only a small step until the object, the subject was taken out of art and the sole items of concern for the suprematists, both the abstract and the concrete painters, was elementary geometry, with occasional excursions into analytical geometry or topology, but otherwise primary school geometry, where all you needed was a compass and a ruler.

resistance to this art was substantial. partly it came from the artists' own circles, as from marcel duchamp and hugo ball, partly there was a sense that the west had been betrayed. there was a rebellion against the loss of the happy medium. but it is over now, the thing is there. there is not a single façade without a piece of cylinder section. museums are turning into slices of cake and coffee machines are becoming rib cylinders. the thing is ingrained.

and we are making sacrifices. eating with cutlery in the basic forms of elementary geometry must suffocate any conversation at table. you have to concentrate on picking up the food. we have never before been asked to sit as uncomfortably as we do today, where a chair has to be a structure of circle segments, squares or triangles, in sheer metal wherever possible. the word sacrifice can be taken quite literally here. you could quite easily need cotton wool to staunch the bleeding, or an elastoplast. the satisfaction remains, you're sitting on art, eating with art.

in fact the relationship between object and ceremonial, between art and religion is evident. periods of atheism need their worship as well. for some paradise consisted of a state with a classless society, others bathed in the purely spiritual empire of geometrical aesthetics. both piet mondrian and wassily kandinsky wanted to provide something more than museum pieces. they wanted to help to conquer materialism and win mankind over to the purely spiritual. this can be read up.

now we eat spiritually, we sit spiritually.

once art served religion, by literally opening up heaven, in the baroque period, for example. in ceiling paintings you see the beyond and eternal peace between the clouds. if you eliminate religion from society, contents may change, but worship remains. and so today churches have been replaced by museums. we sit in worship and eat in worship.

in fact our cutlery would be well suited for liturgical purposes, entirely suitable as sacrifical implements for some ritual. nobody would be able to take offence at that. ritual makes everything sacred, nonsense and possibly inhumanity as well. ritual also conquers the joy and pleasure of eating by forcing us to eat with a kind of toothpick.

neither does anybody take offence at a door latch consisting of a square surface, so long as there is a single cross on this square, a door-bolt for a church.

in terms of present-day perceptions religion relieves us of the obligation of using our heads, having to think. religion is, according to the zeitgeist, pure feeling, the purely spiritual. it is therefore all the more beneficial for the application of services and utensils, which are devoid of all reason. the dignity of the altar permits it to forget sense and purpose as something materialistic, as something profane. only the profane has meaning, and whatever has meaning is profane. the purely spiritual, art, begins only beyond the profane.

then form becomes pure form and principle becomes pure principle. so plato was right. for him body and material were lowering, something dirty. he could not come to terms with his present and fled into the beyond. here in this material world there are purposes, and no ideas.

now it doesn't hurt to take a picture by kandinsky to pieces and make the segments of circles, triangles, rods and squares into neckwear and earrings.

but if you make a set of cutlery to such simple spiritual principles as those represented by circle, triangle and square? then there are only two possibilities: either you sacrifice yourself to the spiritual or you abandon your reason, you give up every intellectual claim in the form of a critical appreciation. cutlery like this no longer makes sense. then the only question is whether it is beyond anything that makes sense or whether it is senseless. of course there are things that transcend the rational that are not accessible to reason, but not everything that is devoid of all reason can get away from the fact that it is merely silly.

the answer that is given today is familiar to us. the cutlery makes no sense, therefore it is art. if we raise eating to the status of art, to a ceremonial, then we are close to god again.

you can bet that this cutlery sells well! at least it will be bought by every museum and every collection that has an "applied art" department, or a "zeitgeist" department.

and now we also have a kettle with the highest possible claim to being aesthetic, but which at the same time cannot be used for pouring. it was designed by aldo rossi and therefore had to be in the shape of a steeple with a little flag on it. it is not quite like that, but pretty similar. it consists of a cone-shaped container which is an equilateral triangle in cross-section, and a handle forming a horizontal and a vertical is fastened on to it. the cone is cut through at the top and the upper part forms the lid. instead of a little flag it has a little ball on the top, so that you can get hold of it better.

the thing is devoid of any usefulness. in an age of prestige existence, we know this, aesthetics naturally becomes an end in itself. it is almost indecent to ask about the use of something. today nothing is better suited to self-representation than appearance, aesthetic form. in aesthetics the thing as such appears.

this kettle by aldo rossi is the kettliest kettle ever, it is the platonic idea of the kettle. but it doesn't actually pour. you have to incline a cylindrical kettle through 90° to empty it completely. and even here your hand has to

ferruccio laviani,
cutlery, 1987.

aldo rossi,
kettle, 1984.

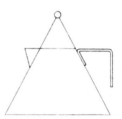

116

make a movement that cannot come from the wrist alone, you have to lift your elbow as well. with rossi's kettle you have to stand up and raise it above your shoulder to reach the 120° inclination that is the least you need to empty it.

and on top of this the kettle has an unfixed centre of gravity. when it is lifted it moves into the corner and makes the kettle difficult to lift at precisely the moment it is almost empty.

but why would you want to pour when the kettle is so beautiful.

we are again living in an age of the ideal. there are values again. mostly even eternal values. there is an entire system of values in which person, family and society form an ordered cosmos. and in this cosmos the ideally beautiful crops up in the form of circle, triangle and square, and lifts our existence on to a higher plane, buildings become pure cubes or cylinders, kettles pure cones. it doesn't matter whether they are any use or not.

in a finer world work is excluded as well. that is left to the staff. celebration of the eternal and the valid cannot take place in the world of work, in the life-world, in the world of living, as it is, it requires a certain élitist exclusion of the public. pouring from a kettle of this kind is left to the butler, who has become modern again, and not by accident. and so this kettle does fulfil a purpose that other, normal kettles do not fulfil. it lets us participate in the ideal cosmos of the eternally good, true and beautiful. the eternal feminine that draws us on does not manifest itself unless you do without asking a woman to cook or bring up children.

yes, the 20th century has sunk as low as that. the kettle as kettle, something you should be able to throw away, has been elevated to the altar of purposelessness, of the pure idea, of pure aesthetics.

aldo rossi is master of the art of the quotation in fusing rationalism with the medieval italian city, just as michael graves' architecture marries frank lloyd wright's to ancient egypt, just as ricardo bofill has married modern concrete building to the architecture of louis XIV, or charles moore occasionally marries adolf loos' work to ancient rome. the age of restoration is categorized by a dialogue with history, at least in the form of the quotation. someone like oswald mathias ungers would be worth only half as much if he had not related the pure cube to charles rennie mackintosh with his graphic art nouveau architecture. it is probably not a real dialogue, otherwise one would want to learn from history as well.

the quotation is enough to prove that the world as it is can no longer be understood and that one feels called to better things. and better things, this is an old belief, are to be found in the past, which, if it is old enough, is even on the same plane as the divine.

the triangle and the medieval spire, that is already more than just playing with triangles. with this aldo rossi also accommodates the art historians of today, who have forgotten how to see a thing as a thing but look for symbolic content and talk in comparisons all the time. they are certainly convinced that aldo rossi's kettle looks like a virgin of the protecting cloak or like a mother hen hatching her eggs or a neolithic prince's tomb. not only because art historians normally know nothing about things - they cannot paint pictures or build houses or design a coffee cup - they talk predominantly in comparisons. this also establishes references to history and to higher things. if they understood anything about things they would have to talk about things, and thus address the question of whether you could pour anything from rossi's kettle or not. but if you talk about higher things you avoid a compulsion of this kind and it also helps that aldo rossi's kettle is selling. its value lies precisely in the fact that it has none. thus in a wonderful way it enriches the furnishings of all our yesterdays and becomes an outstanding element of prestige existence.

but why talk about cutlery and kettles when we are dealing with door handles. there was a first unusable door handle before the first unusable cutlery. it emerged on 20 september 1986 at a design event organized by the franz schneider company in brakel. they had invited a number of designers who are in the news today to develop new shapes for handles. there were nine submissions with a large number of variants.

they included the one that has been described already, which could have been a design by a diocesan building administration, responsible for modern church building.

when confronted with this handle the first thing you ask yourself is: is this an object with a pivot at all, an object that can be pushed? if this object were not attached to a door, but perhaps on a sheet of chipboard that could be hung up, then it would be a work of art. it in fact consists of a square with a squared tube angle to the top and to the side. and anything square is one of the three basic forms of twentieth century visual phenomena of the mind and spirit. a square is pure form, and therefore art. it is true that there is nothing square on the whole of the human body, the square does not appear there, and certainly not as part of the hand which uses or is intended to use door handles. but we know that the body is material, something unspiritual. it is looking for the purposeful.

can you use a door handle with your head, the seat of the mind? who knows, perhaps that will be possible tomorrow. but for the time being we still use our hands to open things. and so is it not perhaps possible, if such a prosaic question might be allowed, that the handle should be suited to the hand?

obviously not. this handle is a sign. it shows a square, divided into further squares. the message is: a square can be divided into sub-squares. but would not a handle, when you are confronted with it, send out the message: i am a handle, please touch me, you can open the door with me?

but that would be a much too normal message, it would have no meaning, no semantic dimension, and thus it would not be possible to include the latch in the current discussion about semiotics. and that would be a pity.

and so the door handle with which i am confronted is a sign of a particular kind. the message cannot be a practical invitation to use the door handle practically. i confront the handle and try to find its meaning, its semantics, as it is called today.

in fact, if i stand still and do not go through the door through which i wish to go, then i realize a thing or two.

casimir malevich comes to mind. he was the first person to paint a picture on which there was only a square to be seen, or rather two pictures, one with a white square on a black ground and one with a black square on a white ground. after the jugendstil artists, like gustav klimt for instance, had very often used the square as a decorative ground, a book by friedrich schumann appeared at the end of the next century in which the square was presented as a primeval form. at that time the cosmos still had basic forms of an elementary geometrical nature in the manner of mandalas. today we no longer know what kind of shape the universe is. but from ancient times to Jugendstil it was spherical.

and so i am faced with a primeval form. and i understand why mondrian or abstract and concrete painters started to paint squares on pictures with a square format. now obviously i have problems with primeval forms. why is an egg not a primeval form, why are there no painters that paint eggs on eggshaped pictures? and there is the additional point that eggs seem to me to have more complex and therefore more clever geometry than the circle, which we have all dealt with in our very first geometry lessons. but we are getting away from our square as a latch.

i know that peter eisenman, who designed this door handle, is an architect. he prefers his buildings to have square ground plans. like tadao ando in japan, for him the cube with sides of the same length is the ideal body. and so buildings with a cubic grid structure are built. and stairs have to be placed in a room at an angle of 45°. certainly ideal stairs, as far as human beings are concerned, have a shallower angle with a relationship of about 2:3. but in spiritual terms a flight of stairs must rise in the proportion 1:1, and has to be a diagonal in a square.

eisenman is not opening just the world of painting for me, but that of architecture as well. i am with palladio, with bernini, and wander through the ages to the architects of rationalism. i perceive myself as a cultural being.

is there any wonder that at first a door with a handle like that doesn't get opened at all? we go away with our tails between our legs because we understood semantics as semantics, as an indication of the thing, as against a proclamation of the "significant".

the "significant" that appears here is the attempt to make an "idea" into reality. this "idea" is the notion of pulling everything in a building together into a unit by means of the same formal design, to make it into a gesamtkunstwerk. in this way the square becomes a supreme, if not a divine principle. from ground plan to door handle, from window opening to lavatory bowl everything is governed by the square. as far as the latter is concerned, the same point needs to be made as was made about the hand. here too there is no square counterpart in a body to designed reality.

alessandro mendini submitted walter gropius' door handle as a design in the door handle competition, only altered in terms of colour, made poppier. but it was not gropius' most mature achievement. certainly the handle consists of a manageable cylinder. the hollow of the hand rests upon it very well. but index finger and thumb get involved in a definite conflict zone of opposing formal concepts. the angle of the handle consists of a four-sided tube with a square cross-section. the point of transition from square tube to cylinder is just at the point where index finger and thumb land when getting hold of the handle.

but o god, if mendini had had a crack at this problem! if he had started to examine the relationship of handle and hand. in an area where something crucial happens, where thumb and index finger are guiding the moving hand, he would have found himself right in the middle of a conflict at the point where a decision for or against reason has to be made. what does a handle look like that gently brakes the thumb and leads the index finger precisely into the inner angle? i have myself addressed this problem both practically and theoretically and can tell you a thing or two about it. the point of contact between artefact and hand cannot be solved with art notions. anyway, i would have submitted a different handle, even if it had not borne the great name of gropius.

nevertheless it must be noted that there are things to be said in favour of the gropius handle. it has its positive aspects.

there is a handle by a düsseldorf designer that i would consider definitely unusable. it is quite obvious that its cultural concept was to make one of kandinsky's pictorial elements into a useful item.

in kandinsky's twenties' paintings there are a lot of geometrical snippets spread around the surface of the picture, including hovering circular segments that look like slices of lemon. at the time this figure contained a so-called tension between the circular bow and the straight line, not dissimilar to the tension of a real bow for shooting.

ergonomics could help to evaluate this handle. but that would be too much of a good thing. it is enough to ask the kind of child who can only see one thing in the fairy-tale about the emperor's new clothes, and that is that the great man was parading around in his underpants.

imagine that you offer a child several hammers to knock in nails, one with a handle with a circular or oval cross-section, one with a wedge-shaped grip and then a few more with handles in flat or raised strip iron. which will be picked up? certainly only the one made of the rounded material. and now, in the case of the instrument with which the door is opened, am i intended to take hold of a wedge-shaped structure as provided by the düsseldorf designer?

this is rather like trying to convince someone that you should take hold of a knife by the sheath and not the handle. and quite obviously you should take hold of the handle correctly, there are guiding ridges on the lower edge for the hand to grip. but you do not take a door handle in your hand, as the language suggests (german: türdrücker, door presser), otherwise it would perhaps be called türgriffer (door gripper). you simply press it, index finger and thumb show the way, and the ball of the hand simply presses down. it's called a drücker. so what are the gripping grooves at the bottom for?

and it is additionally advisable, should you wish to bring a breakfast tray into the bedroom on sunday morning, to take off your outer clothing. the door handle is pointed like a dagger at the back and the front and you could easily get caught up on it if you try to open the door with your elbow.

that this handle is more of a weapon than a useful object is also clear from imagining a device like this fixed to a car. the designer would be in court after the first accident.

rationality and suitability for a purpose cannot be removed from the world more subtly than this. you are faced with a three-dimensional object, a work of art with a central message: function is indecent. sculpture of this kind no longer seems unknown. it has already existed, in the world of naum gabo for instance, or the minsk suprematists.

nevertheless, as a work of art this handle has something attractive about it, it does not consist of a circle, as doctrine would have it, but of a segment of a circle.

mario botta, also one of the new door handle designers, makes do with a circle alone for one of his suggestions. he makes an iron strip into a circular bow. though it is broken to leave the hand a (not entirely safe) slit if it should somehow suddenly be possessed with doubts about how a thing like this is to be tackled at all.

this twentieth century has provided us with any number of revolutions, civil wars and battles. "on to the last conflict" was the watchword every time.

we have to look this fact in the eye. the last conflict is now a possibility. the last reason for a high level of armament is to be found in the fact that the earth can obliterate itself. and politicians are allowed to play politics with this state of affairs.

but the sell-out of reason, a kind of last conflict, is also proclaimed in by objects and objectless door handles, useful items that can no longer be used. life is to become as pure as art, as functionless aesthetics. for this purpose thinking has to be abolished. it is not permissible to be faced with a door handle and to know what it is for as well.

here our Century has demonstrated the link between culture and economics, laid bare the link between body and
soul, demonstrated the link between function and
appearance, between material and aesthetics, and ultimately the cry goes up that all that exists is pure spirit
and pure aesthetics, art consisting of circle, square and
triangle. and even a door handle must be so kind as to fit
in with this.

in defence of the organizer of this design demonstration it must be said that there were other, in part interesting designs, that tried to come to terms with the
designation of hand and handle, but that does not
impinge upon the "zeitgeist".

perhaps i am reading too much intellectual effort into
things here if the first rule of all is to leave your intellect
in the cloakroom?

correct, probably one simply wants to know how much
you can pull a society's leg before it notices that its leg
is being pulled. or do people even believe in what they
are doing?

that would certainly be bad: the end of humanity
because their heads have been switched off. a last battle.

but the world is coming to an end with distinction. the
share of art has increased to such an extent. long live the
triangle, the square and the circle. the gloss is getting
serious.

assume that you have a picasso hanging up at home, a genuine picasso. you could have been a friend of the painter's. that would have meant you might have got hold of a picture by one of the world's most expensive painters, even if you hadn't enough money to buy it. and then you discover that picasso forgot to sign it. the entire picasso would be worth nothing at all. as good as nothing. even if you could show correspondence with him to prove it was genuine, the picture would not be worth anything.

it would seem that it is not longer quality that decides the status of art, but the signature. it is the same with banknotes. they have to be signed by the correct offical in the state bank. according to this, art is not a value in itself, just as little as a banknote. it has a market value. it has, and certainly you have to add: today, a value that is determined by demand from collectors, i.e. by demand from the art trade, by the art business. seen like this, a picasso is a banknote from the art world.

of course this is not an exhaustive answer. there have been periods in art when those who produced art did not sign their work. indeed most artistic epochs did not know the marking of work by appending a handwritten signature. this is relatively new, actually as old as the history of capitalism, which is also a history of the art trade.

in earlier times art was made for a purpose, a person and a particular place. today we are experiencing a blossoming of painting, because it is more mobile than sculpture. painting is as mobile as a banknote, and the principle of trade is not that something is allotted a definitive place, but that it is mobile and can find its way to the place where most is being offered for it.

whether it was an egyptian painter, a greek sculptor or an early medieval wood carver they were creating something for a specific purpose and did not sign their work. occasionally there were marks of origin, of the kind that we know from stonemasons or ancient makers of pottery. designation as personal work, the artist's signature as creator, was not known.

moreover, the signature today is less to identify the creator as a proof of uniqueness, of the original.

only originals awaken the passion of the collector. if there were to be a copy of a picture and even if it was by the same painter it would scarcely be worth half. the signature authenticates the original, something genuinely unique.

the fact that this has led to a new branch of criminalistics only underlines the new significance of the signature.

design is not signed. let us say carefully: not yet. if it were, the inventor of the first electric fan could have become a rich man if he had signed, say, a thousand of the things and marketed them with the care that makes art dear and rare.

but even from its mental attitude design is free of the personality cult of art. design is there for everyone, not for the few and certainly not for individuals. design is intended to be reproduced, duplicated. design hates original and élitist market value. it is looking for the largest possible number of pieces produced and the widest possible distribution.

it is the same as in nature. sunflowers are like sand by the sea. they carry so much seed that their very appearance documents a call for distribution. every bird that distributes their seed is within the meaning of their existence.

a painter who conjures a sunflower on to a canvas makes it into something unique, reverses its nature, makes it into an individual piece. and even if the painter who painted it was primarily painting for himself, even if he was on the breadline, he created the requirement that an individual sunflower is now being traded for millions and millions. it is a requirement that the painter too is an original that indeed van gogh was, that he had a unique brushstroke, so that there can be only one individual who isolated the sunflower in this way.

design is for everybody. it intends to provide optimized useful objects for the largest possible number of people.

what sense would it have made if charles eames had signed his chairs, and gugelot the kodak carousel, nizzoli his lettera typewriter or giorgio giugiaro his fiat uno?

design is anonymous in terms of substance, even if its creators are extremely famous and traded with like couturiers. it is therefore not surprising that there is great design by designers whose names are not even known.

i admire charles eames as a designer. he had his eye on seats as something to sit on, and liberated design from artistic control. today the whole world knows the rietveld chair, which is more like a sculpture by mondrian than an object to sit on. charles eames liberated us from this. and yet i have an armchair, a recliner that moves easily within itself, that is the best that i know in this sector, better than an eames armchair. i do not know the designer's name, and i could not trace it.

and i should not necessarily like to drag him into the daylight. anonymity is noble. i value service to humanity, even if it has remained anonymous. i value the inventor of the bicycle, the pincers, the soup plate, the door latch, lace-up shoes, the steamer, the beer bottle top and the aeroplane propellor. even though we do not know who it was.

and ultimately, who knows who built the city of sienna? he doesn't exist. cities like bern, cultural land-scapes like the moselle valley, appenzell farmhouses, english canals and japanese gardens are collective achievements, but for this reason also not less funda-mental of human culture than the writer of a national anthem.

the most human feature of humanity, its creativity, only has a name in a few cases, and only in the very smallest number of cases can it be identified by signa-ture. we do not even know who built stonehenge, if they existed anyway, and the temple of monte alb·n is as anonymous as the shrine of ise. of what interest is it to us who made the rose window at chartres, the city gate at lübeck or the vladimir dmitri cathedral.

human culture is more co-operative creativity than individual performance (even if victors in battle were always individuals). compulsion towards a cult of person-ality comes from the culture of dominance, where sub-jects were conditioned by veneration, if not worship, of individuals.

who, even, is the creator of our language? it is only through this that we are allowed to think. who changes it, who develops it further? nobody. nobody, because everybody.

if you suddenly come across a designer like johannes potente, and take pleasure in him, and keep finding his tracks, good ones and bad ones, and see how he made his mark on the fifties in particular, then it is not with the intention of dragging him out of the anonymity of history and even making him part of the history of design. he should remain what he always was, an anony-mous designer.

in brakel they have only just found out what design is. johannes potente was surprised that he was supposed to be a designer. he was a worker, made models for door handles, because they were needed and he was that way disposed.

anyone who works for a firm works differently from a designer who would like to have his products shown in the museum of modern art in new york.

johannes potente thought about door handles, not about cultural history. he stayed with the thing, and behaved as trivially as the object deserved. not as though door handles were all the same to him. he lived for them, but only in the context of their use, their construction, their fabrication, not their reputation.

it may be that there are a number of things that he would not have done if he had worked on the basis that humanity, at least its cultural elements, was looking at him. thus he retained uncontrolled casualness. but this very thing is a component of his keenness and evidence of unremitting dealing with the thing itself, not its effect. it is possible that his dialogue with door latches could have been cut off if he had suddenly not been on his own any more, but had design critics looking over his shoulder.

it was not the worst pianists who said they couldn't play in front of big audiences. but they dug the pit of oblivion for themselves. which certainly did not matter to them, for everyone dies one death.

an anonymous designer does not cultivate his style. he does not have one. he is like a craftsman alone in his workshop. he is interested in what comes out. human culture is based on this attitude.

the attitude of power, interested not in the thing but in the effect, and above all in the sublimation of might and influence, does not occur here.

the birth of cities, commerce, traffic, science, technology is based on this concentration on things. cities were built up by many anonymous individuals of craftsmanlike persistence. they were destroyed by great individuals calculating their effect on history. books in academic libraries were written by exponents of hard work and concentration on a subject. they were set on fire by people who wanted to make a name for themselves.

johannes potente from brakel is an example of a designer who put his trust completely in his work. he is not concerned with the problem of what value it has as design as an economic object. he is not responsible for that. he is not even concerned with the fact that in modern industrial society, in our market economy the person who collects all the glory from a product is the person who sells it, not the person who makes it.

modern design is the thing itself. design is a cultural demonstration against decoration, artificial creation of value and historicizing categorization through world style. it emerged from the struggle against 19th century historicism. adolf loos' guiding light was "ornament and crime". he meant that ornament was a turning away from things, betraying the product in favour of appearance and name.

there is something fundamentally incompatible in design and art. each excludes the other, like fire and water.

the creative intensity of design is not less than that of art. on the contrary, making a thing not just beautiful but right as well requires additional creative abilities. art does not have values. art is sense-less. in the sense that it does not need to be sensible it is sense-free. design is measured by things, by their meaning, their social tolerability, their technical function and their economy. art can do without all that.

for this reason mondrian, tatlin, duchamp and even warhol have at one time proclaimed the end of art. life itself was supposed to be the subject of art. they wanted to get out of the culture of sunday into everyday work and invest more creativity there. instead of forcing mankind to worship a cultural heaven they wanted humanity in human beings, pleasure taken in work for its own sake. they remained prisoners of their industry, of the art trade, that kept them on a financial lead. with the exception of tatlin and duchamp. duchamp saw not just the end of fine painting, trying to keep the theme of "l'art pour l'art" alive with paint and canvas, but the end of art itself. at first he discovered aesthetic reality outside the studio. he used objects of industrial triviality. then he rejected art altogether and reduced the energy of shaping something to the subject itself, to the control of one's own life, of everyday humdrum existence, and remained as poor as an ascetic. the art trade had not got him on the lead. but the art trade will have its revenge. it will have a turnover of millions from the few objects that marcel duchamp left behind, because they fulfil the first requirement for high prices, they are rare.

however, nothing has come of the end of art. there would be nothing wrong with that, humanity should paint for as long as it feels like painting and the state should build as many museums for the new freedom as it likes. if it could only continue to be recognized that art and design are two different things. but the zeitgeist wants to have it differently again. it is bringing design back to art.

the value-creating ornament is back on the scene again. bill paints porcelain plates and the backs of clocks. the value-creating factor in art is seizing design. warhol painted cars, and so did calder and lichtenstein.

industry has successfully got itself out of the clutches of not just making and selling products but also of being responsible for them. for this reason it has called for design. products are to be correct, viable, good and beautiful. design had a morality.

design's claims are being repulsed, with the aid of a convincingly simple strategy. products are being artistically garnished again.

seldom has the economy done so much for art as today. care for the eternally good, true and beautiful is its greatest success in fighting off threats from all sides. it simply cannot be excluded any more that mankind could suffocate in the rubbish of industrial society. perhaps we are getting close to a day when there will be no more wars. this is then less a triumph of reason than of the fact that we are compelled to disarm because we need money for the fight against rubbish and the destruction of nature, the destruction of the bases of our own life.

everything and everybody is to blame for this state of affairs, not just those who cause them, industry and the principle upon which it exists, maximization of profit. what is permitted is anything that increases capital.

the economic strategy of promoting art, supporting festivals, symphony concerts and art exhibitions, building museums, setting up galleries, making cultural tourism possible is effective in two directions. on the one hand it distracts from the cause factor, which is that industry, principally the chemical industry but also the motor industry and even the holiday industry, is the first source of the poisons and rubbish of our contemporary civilization. its constant series of new products not only create new waste matter, but also produce a compulsion to consume more and more of more and more industrial output.

then the promotion of culture by industry has an effect that is perhaps even more significant, namely that it makes someone who does something noble seem noble himself. when cortez conquered mexico, an operation that according to hegel cost six million indians their lives, as many as the jews killed under the third reich, he took monks with him as well as soldiers. they preached the gospel, baptised the natives for a new redemption and consequently sanctioned genocide, power politics and imperial violence. power has always used art to have itself justified and to be sublimated by it. large parts of culture have always been power culture, whether in the interest of secular power, of the roman empire for instance, or of spiritual power, the vatican church. why should that be any different today. there is a work of art outside every respectable bank, every respectable office building.

artists usually have a naïve disposition and hardly any of them notice the game that is being played with them. it would not be as easy to do this with sociologists. they still have a sense of the double book-keeping that is done to history. artists like to interpret the role that is played with them as recognition of their art, as confirmation of their mission and as an award to themselves as creative personalities. it doesn't even make them suspicious that people are prepared to spend any sum of money for art.

tom wolfe says that art has become a new religion today. the object it worships is wealth. art sanctions wealth and is itself a source of wealth. art creates capital and secures capital.

one is always overcome by a strange feeling if something that is one of the central issues of history and the writing of history suddenly becomes reality. one does not know whether reality is a dream or the dream is reality. we are all together in the midst of the vortex caused by the dance around the golden calf. we are part of the art frenzy that has grown up around capital.

it is the very cigarette company that is one of the principal causes of the spread of cancer, the very car firm that is considerably involved in atmospheric pollution and the death of the forests, the very chemical concern that has contaminated ground water for generations with its artificial fertilizers, the very major bank that directs the policies of these firms that sets itself up as a patron of the arts, as a sponsor of culture, as a champion of great and pure values. both are interdependent. anyone who produces rubbish needs art.

society and politics seem paralysed in the face of the damage that we have done with our technical civilization. after the nuclear accident, scarcely after it has been cleared up, the hole in the ozone layer comes along, which, scarcely before it has been correctly diagnosed, is overshadowed by the death of the seas. this has scarcely been registered when we discover the chemical contamination of food. everyone says: it is five to midnight, we must do something. then a new tax is discovered, for the little man, for the purification of his sewage. industry, which tips poison into the sea by the shipload, is warned, closely followed by thanks for all

the good things it is doing for art and culture. alongside the seals that are washed up as corpses on the
beaches of schleswig-holstein can be heard the sounds,
sponsored by a few large companies, of the greatest
music festival that has ever taken place.

design is in a difficult position. it is increasingly
betrayed and abandoned by those who were its spokesmen, the representatives of a new, more humane culture.
bestowing a professorial chair is enough to make a critic
of official culture into an admirer of the new sovereignty
of capital. artists can be bought as well.

today's chair is a work of art in bauhaus colours, cut
to shape according to the cultural pattern chart of circle,
triangle and square. furniture is trimmed to size as a
work of art, buildings are chopped down into squares or
triangles. the foundation course with scissors and coloured paper has moved into design offices and studios. a
chair to sit on is too trivial to be permitted a place in the
golden dance. a house to live in is too unimportant, cutlery for eating too superficial, a bed to lie on too rational. everything that is has to become a symbol, a symbol
of the higher, the deeper, leading beyond comprehensi-
bility, beyond reason.

anyone who can invests his money in art. a number of
art magazines leap forward to give advice. art is the best
of all value-enhancing currencies. although this is only
for as long as there is a market for it, as along as there
is some interest. and so museums are built. art is dis-
played at fairs as only cattle, building materials and
machines used to be. sales must be promoted. artists are
quoted and offered like shares. the magic flourishes.
everyone buys, collects, and offers in exchange. the
branch is booming. the only requirement is that the signature is not forged.

people who have to know say that a third of modern
art is forged. we now have better noldes than nolde
painted, better braques than braque painted. if one takes
the judgements of the art world seriously.

and so the person who has a genuine picasso at home,
but without a signature, could quite well forge a signature. in this case it would only confirm the genuineness
of a picture. in this case forgery would actually be the
truth.

intelligent building

modern architecture is based on a programme of social reform. its intention, so it was said, was to bring light, air and sun into every home. people were opposed to dark street gorges, back-yard architecture and bourgeois windows with so many layers of curtains that the rooms were in semi-darkness.

le corbusier's pavillon suisse in paris in 1930-32 clearly set out the counter-position. its entire south side consists of a glass façade, of large windows reaching from floor to ceiling and occupying the full width of the rooms behind it. my first visit to paris, shortly after the war, was to see this building supported by a very few central piers. i sensed that this architecture was proclaiming a new age.

there was one disappointment still to come. in the rooms behind the windows the air was warmed up far too much by the sun and had become stuffy. it was too bright to work in when the sun was shining. everything was light and shade, there were no transitions.

on the basis of this experience le corbusier later added a brise-soleil to his buildings, protruding concrete sunshades, intended to let light, but not direct sunlight into the interior. but the view out of the windows seemed to be enclosed in blinkers.

mies van der rohe's farnsworth house also fell victim to an ideology. it consists of glass panes reaching from floor to ceiling. the light and shade are controlled by curtains. but interior curtains produce a great deal of accumulated heat, which can only be tackled with enormous air conditioning plants.

anyone who knows the desert knows that the southern sun can be a murderous enemy, like the biting cold of the north. an enlightened, time-conscious denizen of the north wears shorts in the desert and a short-sleeved shirt. the experienced camel nomad wears a robe reaching to his feet and also covers his face and head with a cloth. and this is not because he is losing his sense of nudism. we each have a different relationship with the sun, according to where we live. and it makes sense that even prehistoric settlements in italy had narrow alleyways and tall houses, to create shade. narrowness is not just an evil. it can be intentional.

the northern house is a thick-walled climate castle with incised, rather small windows. this encourages awareness of a dualist world. in terms of insulation technique this is a successful solution, but probably only in this respect. was it good to divide the world into strange and one's own, into object and subject, into outside and inside?

in contrast a japanese house is a house without dividing walls to the outside. inner world and outer world are one. whether it rains or the sun shines, the house guarantees movement to and fro between house and nature. on the dividing line there is a fluid transition in the form of a surrounding, raised balcony under a broadly protruding roof. if it is necessary to close the house up because of heat, light or people looking in, paper-thin screens are used. this is the basis of a unique way of perceiving and seeing the world, a personal interpretation of what there is. for example, it became part of zen philosophy, with a particular understanding of dialectic and polarity. for the west there is always the highest, the unique, the only truth, the supreme being, the primeval force, the world formula by which everything can be explained, the state as the crown of society. in japan reconciliation predominates, the balance of opposites. the art of allowing diversity to develop predominates. the traditional japanese house is open from the inside outwards and from the outside inwards. it takes and gives. it is transparent.

obviously the old masters of modern building had something similar in mind, a dissolution of the division between inside and outside, when they started to realize façades as glass walls. but at first there were only ideological solutions, and none that were also technically and physiologically satisfying. windows as a potentially intelligent solution appear in embryo and as successful solutions to parts of the problem, but not yet as a satisfying whole. in individual cases there is ideal protection from the sun, like variable awnings, there are wonderful opening systems for sliding, tilting or swing windows, there are adjustable slatted blinds that can be raised as sight screens, and also as protection from the sun if they are outside. we still do not have the window façade as a totally variable system for all window functions to this day. there are only initial attempts. the need to abolish the gulf between outside and inside has been recognized.

but let us assume that we want a space that is open to the outside in the sense of a world feeling of transparency, in the sense of a philosophy of interconnection and balance. the borderline, the window façade cannot be a façade of large shop window panes as in the work of mies van der rohe. it is a highly complex structure that has to do justice to a wide variety of requirements. it would almost have to be a machine.

three parameters have to be fulfilled. first, this structure must be flexible enough to let sunlight into the space and also protect it from the direct rays of the sun. then there has to be screening. sometimes you might not want to be overlooked, sometimes you might want to see the full panorama outside. human activities assume different levels of intimacy. this means that light itself, even when it is raining, should be subject to control. it's not just the person who likes a lunchtime nap during the day, people who are working should be able to alter and control light as a stimulus to work. slatted blinds, corresponding to the bamboo rolls of the far east, are almost ideal for this. the only thing is that light control must be separated from the provision of shade, otherwise conflicts occur. if you have only one slatted blind or one extended sunshade or one awning to control, clashes occur if at the same time you require an open view but shade from the sun, or an open sky, but protection from being overlooked. if i use a slatted blind to make shade, i can't look out any more, if i use it to prevent being overlooked i do not have any unbroken light.

a window façade as an operational object affords both protection from the sun, ideally from outside, so that there is no accumulation of heat, and also protection from being overlooked, ideally also suitable for varying the interior quality of light, from dark or half-dark via subdued to full light.

if one thinks of controlling light with slatted blinds, two zones should be used from the point of view of height: one up to door height and one closer to the ceiling. these zones should be open to variable control by separate blinds. protection against being overlooked is sufficient to door height, above that you may want things completely open from time to time.

sensitive activities, like designing or writing, require light qualities that can be controlled. to this extent the various layers of curtaining in middleclass drawing rooms, including brocade curtains producing complete darkness, were not a show of pomp. people were in a position to regulate the light in the room in accordance with light moods in the course of the day. this can be done better today. we are becoming increasingly aware of the fact that light, like air, has a broad spectrum of qualities. different countries even have different light. the light of greece has always been recognized as having a specific quality. it is different from the light of ireland or egypt. the lighting scenario in a forest also gives us an idea, especially in the differentiated play of light and shade, that light does not equal light. and morning has a different light from midday or evening. awareness of light is growing, and with this the need to control it.

the third parameter is ventilation. fundamentally a room without windows that can be opened is a physiological cage. air from an air-conditioning system is like air from a tin. air is a high-quality stimulus factor. an airconditioning system can never produce the fresh, tingling air of rain in the country or the dry working air of a summer morning or the soft air of an august evening. it would be ideal if the whole window façade could be opened, either on to the garden or, if you live in a higher storey, out on to a balcony or a terrace. for this you need folding doors. often wings opening above the height of the parapet are enough. but wherever possible opening windows should go right down to the floor. the space becomes freer, outside and inside can correspond better, even if you don't have a balcony or a terrace outside the window façade. even in new york the window reaching from the ceiling to the floor is legitimate. even when it doesn't have opening wings the size of doors. then you just have normal-sized opening windows. even in the case of very tall skyscrapers where extreme wind conditions can occur and people are inclined not to tolerate any opening windows at all, i would not go without at least a few, to make me aware of air as a fluid.

even if windows are kept closed for reasons of temperature people want ventilation that can be adjusted by using window vents. it must be open to sensitive regulation in bedrooms, for instance. anyone who sleeps very awarely has his cult of ventilation regulations according to climate and season. even in cold weather he needs an opening, even if it may be only a tiny slit to freshen up the air he breathes. the zone between door height and ceiling is best suited for regulation of this kind. as today even middlerange cars have electric windows, it should be possible to devise technical equipment that would ensure suitable variability for both tilting and sliding windows. this technical comfort must also be right for slatted blinds. it is not a good sign of technical civilization if control technology is to be found only in the world of industrial work or on the dashboard of a car.

this technology would not have to deliver more than was done by hand in a traditonal japanese house, and that is to provide complete flexibility as far as protection from the sun, protection from light and ventilation are concerned, but today an approach in the direction of making the window façade into a three-sector aggregate is no longer excessive.

seen in this way, the window façade changes from a two-dimensional pane into a three-zoned apparatus staggered in terms of depth. outside is protection from light and sun, that can be completely withdrawn, but also guarantees protection from direct sunlight.

for reasons of insulation technology the actual window façade is a multilayered structure to protect against cold, but against heat as well. integrated into it are opening mechanisms for tilting, sliding or wing openings.

a third zone within the space houses light protection and light quality and light intensity controls. the division of this zone must guarantee that individual windows or doors can be opened without having to move something like a closed sight protection device upwards or to the side.

the apparatus produced for this will contain numerous mini electric motors, like a car, justifying a little control console of their own. building technology is far from advanced in this respect. there are already programme consoles for artificial light that control when where and which lights should go on and off. daylight and ventilation of the space present even more justification for a similar effort.

as i have said, i do not yet know a working example of a window façade of this kind, to say nothing of the appropriate control devices, but starts have been made on individual items.

if one considers the high standard of insulation technology today, it is possible to achieve the status of the japanese house even in colder climates and nevertheless be able to tuck oneself away, as in the traditional western house.

while architecture is concerning itself with problems of this kind it is possible to talk about intelligent architecture. this as a kind of counterposition to so-called modern architecture. modernism was ideological but not intelligent. the cry for light, air and sun was interpreted formalistically rather than technically after the first world war, when this architecture came into being. the one thing the living machine was not was a living machine. the 19th century had established technical architecture with its engineering buildings. with the so-called modern architecture of the 20s an attempt was made to work more in terms of art, to combine technology with aesthetic doctrines like that of circle, triangle and square. this architecture was still familiar with the bourgeois requirement of autonomous art, superordinate laws of pure aesthetics. thus it also saw technology more aesthetically, as a new freedom to fulfil old needs with new means and new materials. buildings had to look like pictures by piet mondrian or amédée ozenfant. they had to be cubes like suprematist art. flat roofs were an aesthetic requirement.

seen in this light the hour in which intelligent architecture was born was norman foster's sainsbury centre, which curves a flat roof just enough to allow the rain to run off.

our much-praised post-modern architecture on the other hand, which only concerns itself with window divisions and bars in the spirit of mackintosh's aesthetics, is regression to naïve formalist playing around. an architect like oswald mathias ungers reduces the problem of the window to pure bar distribution. the distance from solutions that are physiologically and technically satisfying has increased again. if you go into one of the fashionable glass spaces you are often flung back by the enclosed air and greenhouse atmosphere. glass and frameworks are in, the dernier cri of fashion. controlling the climate inside won't bother architecture. lighting technicians, air-conditioning experts and heating engineers are there to do that. the architect slips away from it all into the realm of beauty.

and so we are still waiting for more humane, intelligent building, that finally distances itself from glossing things over, priggish handwriting and gestures that are merely pretty. the architecture we need today has still to come. for it technology is an instrument, not just a storehouse of up-to-date aesthetic structures.

my workspace does not yet exist

i know what a kitchen should look like. i have written a book about it. but i am only slowly becoming aware what my workspace should look like. so far architecture has only provided general spaces for work, well lit, well ventilated, big spaces, small spaces, but no specific spaces.

i know a specific working space from my own neighbourhood. it is an old mill, now an inn. the entire mill was a large space with built-in galleries fitting into the overall space as mezzanines. sacks of corn used to be brought up by lift. then the corn went through various working stages of threshing and cleaning to the millstone, and finally, in the form of flour, down into the waiting flour sack, which itself was also at a height that meant it could be easily loaded on to a cart.

the miller had to have comfortable access to every piece of apparatus for the vertically arranged working stages, and this produced a tissue of platforms and galleries placed in the larger space like bridges and pulpits.

the mill produced a sense of space that has only been found since in accommodation by le corbusier. it is wonderful to live in a space in which you can look up and down as well as out.

large libraries sometimes have similar galleries and bridges and separate workspaces within the overall space, which make it possible to be within a whole and yet to have an individual, separate workspace.

in office buildings by richard rogers and norman foster similar working landscapes embracing several storeys have come into being, usually grouped around an internal hall, and allowing individual working zones within a whole. they have none of the features of the many-storeyed large-scale offices that i hate, in which you can only see beyond the dividing walls to a little bit left over below the ceiling, which seems to be far too low, even if it is high. in the distance there are sliced windows. in the corners there are rubber plants. the howling end of modernism.

i work only in large-scale offices, seen in a working technical sense. my profession requires me to work with other people. and so i want to be in the same room as them. anyone is permitted to see and hear what i am doing. this is the only way to produce the correct network of work and workers. i want to be in sight of them and not to have to open and close doors to get to them.

everything is there for everyone, and everybody works with everybody else. the only thing that can be responsible for the crack-brained idea of creating individual spaces for everyone and everything is the inferiority complex of officialdom, afraid of a hierarchy of scrutiny.

with the exceptions of toilets and darkrooms i cannot think of a single room that absolutely has to be separate. a separate room for talking about money and personal matters will not be needed in our offices. even if it may be understandable that there is one for this purpose. and why shouldn't my colleagues be aware that i am cursing on the telephone or being especially forthcoming with somebody? there is no secret that may not be known by everyone. i presume that this is the secret of a socially and psychologically intact place of work. when workspaces start to be split up and sealed off then squabbling and bickering begin, privilege, prestige, hierarchy, power, authority. the result is a working world that functions according to the principle of regulation, according to the principle of the military and the state.

but if you want to work in an open working landscape you are faced with real problems. for example people like to have a sense of their own working space, indeed their own working niche that allows them to think as an individual as well, to write, to design and to dream.

i myself have three quite different spheres of activity. i am in charge of an office. this means that i have to hold conversations, either at my colleagues' workplaces, or mine, or around a larger table if several people are involved in the same conversation. i am an entrepreneur. this means that i do business. i usually work this out with my secretary, who is responsible for business arrangements. she keeps a record of my appointments, deals with telephone calls and handles correspondence. her working apparatus is telephone, computer and writing equipment. we even need to be able to see each other. if i hear that yet another journalist wants an interview or to make a film or someone is trying to book a lecture, all to feed a stultified information society, then a wink has to be enough to help her to give the right answer. it's just possible that tom wolfe might be making an appointment.

if i want to get on with my own work i don't want to be disturbed by every telephone call and everything the fax machine spits out. my secretary keeps an eye on this, usually by eye contact. if it is at all possible i avoid speaking to her on the telephone. she would bother me by ringing all day long, i should have to keep picking up and putting down the receiver, when a small gesture that she can see says everything. additionally i always have questions to ask her. and i don't want to telephone or to have to open a door for that either.

telecommunications have made business easier in many ways, but i would be a slave to them if i were to abandon myself up to them completely, as they do not take account of what i am doing at any particular moment. my secretary protects my creative powers against the pathological desire of new technology to be able to get hold of everybody anywhere and at any time. we must have the right to protect ourselves against progress as well.

finally, and this is my third sphere of activity, i am also a designer. i draft, think, draw, write, read, phantasize, develop ideas, reject them and look for new solutions.

a work-place for this must have something of the monk's cell about it. a great deal is pure meditation or concentrating on being stimulated. but at the same time my monk's cell would have to have something of the viennese café about it, in which a man of letters fabricates a text in the middle of the bustle of the city. the greatest concentration often requires the stimulus of being busy, the internal needs the noise of the external. not always. but the enclosed cell is good only if it has an exit to a garden and a cloister.

for me a space in which creative work is possible is not an enclosed space. it can be created by a bookcase or even a lighting track in a room combined with a storage shelf. we have designed such room dividers, principally to create psychological structuring to produce a more private work-place.

an office like ours is a complexly structured thinking workshop. we are a combination of control centre, post office, university institute, monastery and small printing works. this jumble could be better structured spatially, broken up, without breaking or cutting communications. today i can only imagine an architecture appropriate to this on two levels. a single office on two levels, at least two levels.

i was not a little surprised when making studies for office organization of this kind to come across a project by norman foster in which he has foreseen offices like this on two levels: a large space extending over two floors, in which a bridge area had been fitted.

the bridge, fixed free in a two-storey space, is for me the space for thinking, the place for phantasizing, playing, living and working in space, bathing in the dimension of intelligence.

i like looking from the organ gallery into the nave of a church, from a bridge into the docks, from a tree into a meadow. the circle, not the front row is my favourite place in the theatre. the captain works on a bridge above the ship. on the ground or on an office floor you work in two dimensions. a bridge raises us into a consciousness that is richer by an extra dimension. this is the dimension of outlooks and broad views.

a bridge in my office would be a light, articulated platform in the space with several work-places for all creatice activities and all colleagues whose principal activity is thinking. here people search, write and sketch. any drawing produced here is a sketch, it is executed and perfected on the drawing board or the plotter, on the floor below.

the ideas formulated here are hand-written. they are carried out and edited on the floor below. up here the telephone buzzes rather than rings. there are books up here, but only those that are needed for work in hand, the library is down below. the secretaries are down below as well, in visual contact.

one of my greatest discoveries in the last few years is the pencil. the longer and the more i work with a computer the more i discover a new world, the world of the pencil.

in our day the computer has produced two classes of people that are strictly separate. some people work with computers and do what their programmes suggest. they sit casually in front of the monitor, key in a question and wait to see what the monitor says. usually this involves an instruction about what key to press next in order to get any further. this continues until you arrive at a result.

this is the way that bankers and production engineers, but also professors in institutes work.

the other class are based at the other side of the computer. they work in pencil. they are allowed to draft, think, phantasize, enquire, ask questions and sketch out possible answers. this class does not work in a digital world, its members live in an analogous world of things, images, links, thought landscapes and they move as freely as the owl of minerva. they are content with a pencil. their achievement is to formulate a sentence, not its communicative processing. it can be written by hand. their achievement is finding an idea. it can be captured in sketches. it does not have to be captured in a fair copy of the kind necessary for production. they concern themselves with concepts, programmes, drafts, they check and reject on the basis of evaluations of which a computer is not capable. they operate in a free landscape of questions, openness and outlooks, and they examine problems, cases, possible solutions. a piece of paper and a pencil are sufficient for this.

of course they provide feedback for the class of executors, realizers, statisticians, those who prepare and assess production, the people in front of the monitors. but they cannot work to a programme. their advantage and also their destination, their use, is to be free. because without them the computer would run out of programmes.

is the new office an image of this two-class society? are there thinkers and doers on the upper level and servants of the service sector, the stokers of the information society, employees of the computer and administrators of automation on the lower level?

a cynical picture.

but perhaps my office is also a bridge over the gulf that divides the two classes. perhaps there are only a few spiral staircases from the upper level to the lower. but we are all working in the same space. as well as a horizontal structure for the office there is also a vertical one. those on the upper level are dependent on what people do below, they see each other, they talk to each other, vertically as well. and the people below see what the people above are doing. they move up and down.

i think that architecture can contribute in its way to healing the diseases of our times. it needs transparency instead of division, association with colleagues rather than isolation.

but architecture also has to structure the undifferentiated, structure the unit organization. in architecture consciousness becomes concrete. the condition of the times is demonstrated in built form.

my office is a three-dimensional garden with various levels, separate workplaces. the dividing walls have fallen. the various activities take place on various platforms. but the space is an open structure. you can see the people you want to see and hear the people you want to hear. general and public things take place on the lower level. here there are drawing tables, desks, telephones and computers. special things develop on a higher level. here there are ordinary tables, pencils are enough. there are books, everything that you need for thinking.

difficulties for architects and designers

building and design in the twenties aimed to overcome all style and get back to the matter in hand. at first jugendstil began to replace historicism, particularly neo-gothic and the neo-renaissance style of the imperial period, with an up-to-date style, then style as such became questionable. adolf loos, otto wagner and josef hoffmann built the first bare-walled buildings in vienna, whereupon the battle-cry went up: ornament is a crime! le corbusier applied amédée ozenfant's naked cubist forms to building, and gerrit rietveld followed the principles of the de stijl movement.

but it was always formalism. square, circle and triangle were seen as fundamental aesthetic values, whether for lamps, buildings or new typefaces. they were forced into the straitjacket of elementary geometry and were thus supposed to be closest to truth. even constructivism turned out to be style, under closer scrutiny.

it was only gradually, through the initiatives of the werkbund and the later bauhaus that functional points of view moved into the foreground. design became more open. a typeface is easier to read if it has oval characters rather than circular ones; it is better for the reflector of a lamp to follow a parabola than a circle. and a building does not have to have a flat roof at any price, simply to look like a cube.

the architects and designers of germany, russia and the netherlands in particular turned to the programmes and needs of the workers' movement and attempted to use industrial production methods as an economic advantage for building reasonably priced housing. new materials like steel, sheet metal, plywood or concrete were intended to secure better quality whilst at the same time reducing costs by series production. the image of a new society was seen in relation to a new technical culture, and building and design were related to practical problems and concrete tasks concerned with social change.

a building built by an architect in present-day new york in the tradition of constructivism, in imitation of le corbusier for example, no longer has anything to do with this. it would still have a few superficial things in common like a love of right angles and the colour white. today cost is no longer a factor, and so rational production or industrial manufacture are not either. the building is an aesthetic end in itself. you can also live in it.

when el lissitzky visited le corbusier's first buildings in
paris he was horrified by the luxury that was an essential
part of the architect's new building. as a designer of
kitchens amongst other things, el lissitzky saw new
design as directly related to social programmes, to
improving living conditions, overcoming poverty and
inequality among human beings, securing the individual
living space, application of advantages of industrial production to social progress. design was motivated by the
image of a new society, often a utopia. art was no longer
necessary because design of the things of everyday life
and life itself were intended to achieve a quality that
was also aesthetic, as was otherwise customary only in
art. the museum was the street, the factory, the house.

le corbusier and charlotte perriand designed expensive
armchairs in chrome and leather when what was really
needed were ordinary chairs. thorstein veblen had
exposed aesthetic luxury as part of the class struggle, the
most refined weapon in the fight for power and privilege.
aesthetics for its own sake he considered to be the most
noble representation of power.

so from the very beginning modern building and
design were split into a new aestheticism and formalism,
and a functionally orientated social programme. one
group saw circle and square as elementary aesthetic
form, the other as the result of industrial means of production. even karl marx had defined rotation (the lathe)
and translation (milling, rolling) as form-determining
basic movements of technical production.

it is not meant that one group built for the rich and
the other for the poor. what is meant is that one group
stopped at the bourgeois cultural perception of élitist
aesthetics and the other group derived their design from
industrial production conditions and tasks of a new
nature for making a life worthy of human beings possible
for everyone. their functionalism was related to production, materials, construction, use, but also to the nature
of tasks and social aims. this functionalism was a tangled
web of impulses and aims, always connected with the
claim of achieving something ultimately valid in aesthetic
terms as well.

the frankfurt kitchen was another product of this attitude. it was not simply intended for the subjective satisfaction of women, but also applied to their new social
role as someone increasingly involved in the business and
working world. it was produced not as a marketable
range by a kitchen manufacturer, but as a challenge
from architects and town planners who were concerned

about new forms for city estates and integrating the peripheral groups of the 19th century into society.

if one disregards trivial things like rectangular, shar-pedged dishes with handles, there are no elements of the kind of art deco used by the middle classes and the nouveau riche in their interiors that express allegiance to a better culture of circles and squares. the functional aesthetic was open and receptive to appliances like the gas oven and the revolving chair. in the thirties this ingenious aesthetic was then able to develop fully after formal games with circles and squares had been dropped from the field of vision for a little while. gerrit rietveld's cubist chair was no longer in evidence, and seating models emerged that from marcel breuer to charles eames brought a breakthrough of real functional and technical understanding, and at the same time an aesthetic that came from the factory and not from an ideology, convincing and yet new, severe and yet natural. there was no need to take this aesthetic back to some sort of formal code. no such code existed. its source was the thinking of engineers, from now on bound into a demand for proportion, order and law.

today we live in an affluent society, indeed a society of excess and overproduction. our life instinct is put on the same level as consumer instincts and advertising wishes. this means binding the subject into an economic cosmos whose principle of profit maximization has produced an extreme concentration of power. but power is suspect. and the best way of concealing power is still aesthetics. building and product design are again almost exclusively a question of style and thus also a question of fashion. fashions always emerge when form is arbitrary and does not present the information value of a state of affairs. where it does not represent anything it is interchangeable.

nowadays formal concepts of this kind change like the years. architecture in the sense of commitment to its subject matter and for the people who have to use it, as commitment to the correct use, the right application of materials and production methods has become extremely rare. it is part of the declared, rather than the subliminal programme of so-called post-modern architecture to build scenery, dummies and set pieces.

no-one talks about kitchens any more. that would be too trivial a thing in a society that represents, rather than presents itself. art is an industry as well, and just as subject to manipulation and speculation as trading in goods.

after the war the swedish kitchen was still a kind of up-to-date completion of the frankfurt kitchen. the unit wall became complete, division from the rest of the accommodation was reduced by the serving hatch. sliding doors and roller drawers took account of reduced space. kitchen lights with naked bulbs gave way to the fluorescent tube, which developed further into the concealed working light.

current contributions by architects to kitchens are restricted to the occasional kitchen bar, applications of the occasional experience of a hard or long drink in the home area. the best people occasionally have a bar for visitors who enjoy shakes, snacks or drinks.

contemporary architecture is no longer interested in solving problems, it wants to create appearances. like programme music, today's architecture intends to express something, to communicate semantic content. this includes all sorts of indications, but none about the building itself, its content, how it came about and the way it was constructed. architecture is not information about the interior of a building, it is correspondence with other architectures like those of schinkel, vitruvius, palladio or le corbusier. the architect does not see himself as the custodian of a building, but as part of architectural history. his building cites architecture, or is a polemic. fin de siècle games were always like this.

perhaps it is also true that concern with kitchens has been taken from architects by designers. or even by manufacturers. the latter now have marketing departments and know what the market wants. nevertheless the question of the relationship of the kitchen to the living space, what its status in a modern ground plan would be has remained unanswered until today. on this subject robert vorhoelzer, walther schmidt and hanna löw made the last intelligent statement: they tried to use a glass partition to separate cooking and living.

for designers kitchens have become a big thing, for appliance designers as well as system designers.

but our designers are in a bad way. technical civilization has so split up the world of work in contrast with the craft age that the person responsible for research does not bother what marketing is doing, and marketing is not responsible for materials or manufacture. the sales person knows nothing about design and and the designer is not familiar with the way in which the businessman builds up his calculations. in bygone days a wheelwright was still responsible for the technical quality of his product, the way it was processed, the

materials, its appearance and for organizing the workshop. the designer has become a specialist in form who
is the highest court of appeal under the compulsions of
the marketplace. he is responsible for the appearance of
a kitchen, not for its programme and technical quality.
he is there to optimize the market, with others but in
his own way, using colour, materials and arrangement.

designers have made food processors, coffee machines
or bread slicers look good, they have brought refrigerator
and oven to the correct working height, they will also
solve the problems of ventilation and lighting, which
until now have been the poor relations of kitchen development. but where is the designer who could allow himself to question the cutting mechanism in his food
processor or the coffee machine as such? the evenly cut
pieces of lettuce that come out of our modern kitchens
seem not to be standardized goods only to someone who
has never yet prepared lettuce for friends, one finely cut,
the other torn by hand. or sliced, diced, chopped, grated,
a different approach for every kind of vegetable. and
anyone who loves coffee above all else and has perhaps
learned in the arab world to distinguish what is really
good coffee, no longer uses a coffee machine. what
should a designer do - criticize appliances that precisely
he has brought into the kitchen and made an integral
part as the custodian of technical progress? electrical
appliances are a blessing. but which is and which isn't is
no longer a question of design.

if there is reincarnation and everyone has had a previous life, then i was an engine driver in my earlier life. i
love machines, i love technology, i see my life as a construction draft. but i do not like technology for its own
sake. i don't use pliers to pick flowers. and how many
designers are not still dreaming today about a kitchen
with a control panel.

on a panel choosing the best kitchen design the following criteria are used:
- use value (ergonomics, technology),
- design quality (function, construction, innovation),
- integration into the kitchen ensemble (design coher-
ence, appearance).

does this context produce the question of whether it is
viable in terms of working psychology that in principle
only one person can work in modern kitchens? the working
medium and means of leadership of a top manager is conversation. they are rarely seen alone. bricklayers always
work in a team, a bricklayer without a labourer and an
apprentice is a cripple. where possible people work in

groups in the car industry. only kitchens are seen in principle as a one-man business.

this has hurt neither architects nor designers. it is only when the question whether a computer kitchen with a fixed seat as a vantage point would be worth aiming for is asked that the thought crops up that occasionally there is more than one person in the kitchen. otherwise the doctrine of the frankfurt kitchen remains untouched.

in my interviews with chefs from top restaurants i usually found designless chaos, only large-scale kitchens in factory canteens and hospitals were drawn up according to the requirements of modern design. since then i have seen a link between order and boredom and improvisation and initiative.

contemporary kitchens with their design clarity exude an aesthetic of passivity and representation. they are beautiful, but actionless. the aesthetics of action lead to order of a different kind, that of flexibility and mobility. it has the charm and stimulus of chaos: just beware if anything is in the wrong place. order to help initiative and thus improvisation is not a subject for today's design. design is identical with a static aesthetic, with an awe-inspiring appearance that is now appropriate only to art.

afterword

it is certainly possible to think about whether the autonomy of doing things oneself that has been won back in kitchen work possibly releases more freedom than all the great avowals of freedom we bandy about. possibly freedom is nothing large or small. perhaps it is an aggregate condition that comes about through doing - in contrast with speaking of the kind that hovers above the ground - so that freedom begins everywhere where someone begins to touch.

there is a lot of talk today about the freedom that an ecological movement is supposed to bring us. i distrust this too. i do not wish to join in with the great chorus of those who preach against waste but have our rubbish taken away by turks as the new slaves of civilization. ecologists are too good to take away the rubbish they have produced themselves, even if it is only part of it. i mistrust people who attack a cynical industry in the name of nature, but unthinkingly help themselves from it where food is concerned. and it is by no means difficult to strike fear into the heart of the food industry: don't buy ready-made soups, cook them yourself.

it is the same with the state: everybody grumbles about it and feels that it restricts his freedom. but everyone expects it to look after us. they all come running when it hands out honours, and the intelligentsia crowds around with embarrassing vehemence at places where professorships are handed out. almost nobody is too proud to do without state support and get his own provisions for the winter together. everyone expects that a perfect system, a perfect bureaucracy will set up cribs with food everywhere.

if there is one word today that has been worked down to the bone then that word is freedom. so let us not say that even cooking brings a little freedom. let us say that it is fun and can - if done correctly - bring satisfaction to us, our nearest and dearest and our friends.

if a business develops a product or can offer a service, in the end a designer is called in to make the thing more beautiful. in one case he may be a product designer, in another perhaps a graphic designer. let us call this an additive design. it has something to do with arranging clothes. animals are always dressed. human beings are naked and add working clothes, leisure clothes or evening dress.

in a similar way entire businesses have started acquiring clothes. a cigarette manufacturer buys a symphony orchestra, a bank acquires a collection of modern painting, a car manufacturer runs an art gallery. the mantle of culture that one adopts has advantages. it is attractive to the outside and it covers up on the inside.

it remains to be seen whether this is questionable, reprehensible or useful (probably it is all three). it is different in the case of companies like ERCO or braun. there design is part of the purpose of the enterprise. the product would not be what it is if it had not been seen as a design object from the outset. design is a drafting principle and its demands, criteria and methods determine the product as a whole, not just its surface.

since the renaissance we have considered the world predominantly in terms of perspective, as a phenomenon. in doing this we have lost the thing itself to some extent. when an architect designs a building he has to draw geometrically, not in perspective. he has to catch the structure, articulation and construction of his building. in the last resort appearance is something that comes out, that emerges. it is a result, and has perspective only as a result.

there is such a thing as surface design, cosmetic beautification, and perhaps design is more and more interpreted in this way. at ERCO design goes into the product, use and aesthetics are developmental criteria alongside technology and usefulness from the beginning.

they are not dealing just with the product itself. any work is at the same time a general test of whether one is on the right lines overall and whether technology or design should not be further developed as a whole. one sees oneself as a workshop in a world-wide cultural, technical and economic context.

any business that is design conscious in this way, and aware that design is more than a pretty dress, and at the same time also aware that its own design is an element in general design development, profits from it and gives it impetus, a company of this kind also has its own perception of what is known as visual appearance, its corporate identity. it is not just the visual image of the entire company in the sense of a suit, it is an attitude, just as reagan and gorbachev show a different attitude whatever they are wearing. character and personality have a visual appearance as well.

and additionally, the visual appearance of ERCO is an object of reflection. it is related to similar efforts elsewhere, and it is related to the question of what a company is at all today. one can ask oneself: mustn't businesses today think an ecological size bigger, just as they once had to learn to grow a social dimension bigger? in the same spirit one can also ask: is the company of today not dependent on a culture of self-presentation, emerging from itself? companies originally saw themselves as "mercantile" enterprises. they have grown into a social balance. today they have to expand by adding the horizon of ecological morality. will they not have in principle to develop further to be companies with their own culture of what they do and how they appear? corporate identity is booming.

in fact, everything that is has shape, and why shouldn't institutions as well have a face. as early as the fifties there was a wave of concern about outward appearance and outward manner in the name of image and imagemaking, but this was more from the point of view of cosmetics and tailoring, conscious style-making and finery. "image" soon adopted the negative connotation of cultivating a trendy appearance. and when even politicians talk about how they should do more for their "image", and when financial institutions expect a colleague's appearance to be appropriate to the concern and not so much to the person, there is not much to it.

in fact, everything that is has its shape, its gestalt. even something as amorphous as the wind is revealed as an artful current when you see its cloud picture in the satellite photographs that are daily put before our eyes. even something as intangible as feelings develop their own gestalt. you can see whether someone is grief-stricken or contented. unlike aristotle, who distinguished a thing's substance, which is essential, from its accidence, which is casual and external, we have to see the external as a picture of the internal.

in reality there is no outside and no inside. you can tell from any child's face whether it is lying or telling the truth. usually the first impression of a person is the clearest as far as assessing character, attitude and nature are concerned.

shape is no longer to be seen as external appearance, but as a picture of the whole. daisies and sunflowers are what they are, in their picture. bull and cow reveal their nature in their appearance. man and woman are also in essence as they appear.

if we leave aside the fact of camouflage or mimicry in nature, where it is a matter of making oneself invisible to an enemy by adapting oneself to one's surroundings in colour and shape, man is the only creature who is given the opportunity to give himself an artificial shape, in analogy with his ability to make tools and project an enlarged personality into his surroundings by means of artefacts. he not only shapes his tools, his prostheses, his extensions, but also himself.

shape is not just picture and outline, shape is also, in the dimension of time, manner, gesture, behaviour. one looks like one is and one acts as one is. this relationship is so close that the converse is also true: people take on the character of their manner and become the picture that they make of themselves. you can even adopt model pictures. but they are not so much a likeness, a mere appearance for behaviour worthy of imitation, but a guiding principle for orientation, attitude and character. model pictures are the first orientation towards finding oneself.

people are as they show themselves and as they show themselves so are they. the visual image is not just external, although it is seen as such by many according to classical philosophy. it is the actual thing. one cannot exist without showing oneself and as one shows oneself so one is.

this makes the question of the visual image first and foremost a philosophical and moral problem. it does not lead first to the problem of clothing, of fashion, of manner. it leads to the question of existence. who am i? this is the crucial question of self-presentation. thus we are dealing with three phenomena

– there is appearance, gestalt as a presentation form of character, thing, content, appearance and thing are identical.

– there is a conscious shaping and change of this basic gestalt in the sense of mimicry, of diving down into environment and surroundings. shape is extinguished.

– conversely there is accentuation of appearance in the sense of introducing symbols, of seeking to be striking and attract attention. this is served by such established institutions as fashion or advertising.

the problem arises questionable when point three starts to become independent and no longer relates to point one, when shape as symbol starts to move away from shape as thing. in a world of perspectives and views, of surfaces and façades, of manner and show this almost becomes the rule. world theatre becomes the theatre world.

in the fifties, not altogether stupidly, after bad experiences with the concept "image", we introduced the concepts "visual appearance" and "projected appearance" as a pair of concepts to be allotted. anyone talking about his visual appearance should also talk about projected appearance. projected appearance is the image of how one would like to look oneself. visual appearance is the visible form of projected appearance, its concretization in gestures, behaviour, attitudes, profiles, lines, styles, in colours and figures, in actions and achievements, in products and objects.

projected appearance helps people to come to terms with themselves. today people would say that they had found their identity, were at one with themselves. the basic problem of morality. the visual appearance is the shaping and development of this coincidence.

the aicher office, which has existed since 1946, was probably the first german graphic design office to concern itself with visual communication in the sense of visual appearance. instead of offering elaborate advertising, it attempted to derive aesthetic qualities from the fact of communication, and to create for the subject that wanted to communicate itself those semiotic elements that lead to its presentation, to its self-presentation.

the aicher office is an office that sees advertising not as an aesthetic business, but as part of a company's self-projection. this can thus be only part of a comprehensive visual appearance for a firm or an institution.

originally the office produced advertising like any other advertising agency. this meant attractive, interesting, effective advertisements with the aid of particular attention values. certainly this is a craft in its own right requiring special creative abilities, but unfortunately it is usually a matter of self-extolment, which certainly isn't too keen to test itself against credibility. advertising is usually brought in from a distance and often talks past the thing to which it is referring instead of addressing it directly.

how is credible advertising to be achieved? by seeing advertising as part of a firm's self-presentation.

in this way the idea of the visual appearance of a firm became our actual field of work. distinctive visual appearance has the advantage of making a very strong effect outwards without having to resort to verbal self-extolment. we had found a new field of work alongside advertising and graphics, even though we had no concepts for it at first.

the visual appearance of the firm of max braun is still a classic today. they produced their first new radios, kitchen appliances and electrical appliances in 1954. with the exception of the industrial design element, the design of the appliances themselves, the aicher office controlled all the visual elements, which of course meant that individual elements of the appliances also had to be defined, like colours, instructions for use, labelling, position and look of the company mark. in addition it was a question of choosing and specifying the use of typefaces and colours, typographical guidelines, design of printed matter, definition of pictorial communication, exhibitions and exhibition systems, displays and display windows, appearance in the press and in public. the image of this firm has remained substantially the same until today, of course shaped above all by the design of the appliances, which came into being in correspondence and agreement with the graphic design and was based on the same principles.

this was largely mental work. it was conducted in intensive and permanent discussion with the company, design management and the designers. in the course of this the company men crept into the philosophy of the designers and the designers into the philosophy of the company. the outside came from the inside and the inside from the outside. as philosophy was applied to the product, making became philosophy and philosophy became making. both an image and an attitude emerged. this is manifest in the friendships between those involved, which have lasted until today. the success of the enterprise has now long rested on other shoulders. our task was to create a platform.

design is company philosophy made concrete. it shows the company not as capital, possession or labour, but through its products and services.

so far it has been said of a firm's products that on the one hand they have a technical function that determines their performance, and on the other hand a formal function that determines their appearance. this is wrong thinking. just as human beings no longer allow themselves to be divided up into soul, body and mind, the technical element as such is always also an appearance form, a dimension of the technical element. design puts the technical and economic philosophy of a firm into the picture, and the visual image of the firm at the same time becomes its character, determines its mentality. the designer is the philosopher of the company, who, however this may be, brings about its perceptible appearance.

this is certainly something different from what we understand by corporate identity today. critically formulated, corporate identity is looking for useful application of aesthetic fashions and current trends in the interest of market advantage. people also wish to make use of the zeitgeist subservient to economy and harness it to achieve the aims of the business.

but the zeitgeist is external. what would have to be made visible is what is inside, in the company itself.

now every firm is there to achieve economic goals. turn of the century economists, like werner sombart, for example, called this aim maximization of profit.

this can definitely still stand. the question is only how and to what end does one achieve this maximization of profit? and then design is immediately at the centre of entrepreneurial decisions and discussions.

another key project of mine was the visual image of the german airline lufthansa in the late fifties. in this case the design process was not conducted in the boardroom. the firm was too big for that and subject to the traditional system of division of labour. it was not joint intellectual and speculative work as it had been with braun. the board ordered, decided and had things carried out. this showed in the result as well. this did turn out well and essentially still exists today, but it was not the best it could have been, although they established an outstanding design department of their own. the board's decisions were, as board decisions tend to be, outside its own competence and dependent on the inclinations and whims of the board members.

this actually means that original design, original visual appearance can only be developed to full maturity in small and middle-sized firms, even though individual board members may have more competence. this is a structural problem.

businesses can be run to plan like a railway or public services. other businesses have a digital decision-making structure. they live on figures and manage on figures.

there are figures as data and figures as guidelines. the consequence is that qualities are also expressed in quantities. the quality of an enterprise shows in figures on growth, turnover, profit. the performance of an employee is indicated by his salary grade, or the salary grade is an assessment of his performance, whether this is right or not. The quality of a product is determined by its sales, whether this is true or not.

this digitial system is the currently accepted economic management system used by large firms. the introduction of computers and the introduction of mathematical models into the economy should have led to certain prognostication of economic processes, as was initially believed.

it was a disappointment. economic management too is an analogous process, a process of assessment. decisions are not made on the basis of logical conclusions, of rational compulsions and deterministic calculation, but by assessing positions. decisions do not mature in a linear fashion, but by considering a field, in comparing the most different magnitudes that perhaps cannot all be reconciled. relationships and references are drawn, links recognized, and a balanced, not a financially balanced, judgement has to be made.

we have all once believed in logic, but had to learn that it is use that releases useful insights. this was also brought home to us by the branch of science known as cybernetics. cybernetics is a science of control, not of planning. perceptions ripen in the closed loop of cybernetics.

in middle-sized and small businesses there is no bureaucracy in the real sense. bureaucracy is the institution of digital economic management. analogue management is based on perception, on assessing states of affairs as complex situations on one's own authority. only the analoguous way of looking at things is comprehensive and diverse enough to understand and evaluate complex situations.

lufthansa was too big to make design an in-house object. they bought it in, and also made decisions in the way you make decisions about things you have bought in. nevertheless the result was acceptable.

as far as its visual appearance was concerned the company was in a dreadful state, on the level of homemade utility graphics. the aircraft was more like a vehicle for advertising and in visual terms was dressed like a fairground salesman.

our idea was to make the aircraft itself as a technical apparatus and its technical appearance the object of a company presentation. we used only lufthansa'a two house colours, eliminated all decorative colours, ornamental lines and emblems. instead of a combination of lettering and a trade mark we found the lettering, the logogram, was enough. the sign was not to be used, but the board did not support this. the blue appeared in a technically orientated band that held the aircraft's row of windows together. the whole tail unit was yellow. this opportunity to establish an unambiguous colour specific to the company at airports was also not taken. they ended up with a blue tail with the yellow sign, the "fried egg" was born, and this is still an embarrassment today.

our notion that confidence in an airline should come first of all from the aircraft and the projection of technical competence, which would also have contained a clear marking of the services and the organization, was only accepted to a limited extent.

how long does visual appearance of this kind survive?

the braun appearance is still in place today after almost three decades. lufthansa's also still exists. as in this case no unambiguous concept had been reached and we had been subjected to whims over the matter of decision, competitors reached our own standard and even exceeded it. in the late seventies we made suggestions for a modification of the overall concept. it would have been possible to take just a few measures to freshen up the visual appearance and to make the company younger and more competent. we returned to the initial philosophy.

later i read extracts from this philosophy in the press as statements by a new company chairman who found a change in the previous visual appearance acceptable to identify new activities. new brooms sweep clean, and so he got himself a new design team.

corporate identity businesses sprang up like mushrooms in the seventies. advertising agencies found a new sphere of activity here and approached our concept that advertising could only be one aspect of a comprehensive representational and visual appearance for a company. economic journalists, who like dealing with art and aesthetics, spun the subject out and everywhere people were talking about corporate identity, company culture and corporate design. but this was perceived as a kind of accoutrement, like a visit to a couturier or a hairdressing firm, that also provides toupees. the whole thing degenerated into cosmetics, encouraged by a new design concept that saw form as a decorative addition according

157

to the spirit and taste of the times. the product was intended to be a symbol of the times. but what are the times?

lufthansa too was to have a new costume. a kind of canary was born. there was a rebellion, the whole thing was called off. nothing became of the freshening up project. what now remains is a lack of concept, and the company is losing its profile, as can be seen. this too is a pointer, and this is why the example is being named, that visual appearance needs a content concept, its own concept of the firm's philosophy, the development of a projected image. being measured for a new suit doesn't make you a better person.

for this reason we once refused to design a new visual appearance for BMW, because here the product philosophy of the super-fast, super-powerful car, the sofa as a rocket, would have been in the way. for this we would have had to have thought of something just as pubertal and trendy, but it wouldn't have fitted in with the realities of today's traffic. divergencies showed in preliminary thinking about the car of the next decade. additionally the car is an object of worship that also needs a kind of altar design.

these are a few cases. it would be possible to say something in principle about every design that we have developed over the years, which may make it clear that the visual appearance of a company in all its recognizable forms is more than beautification or involvement in current cultural trends. it is never possible to superimpose visual appearance, it has to be developed from the thing itself. we gave a publishing house clear and effective design and layout in this way by thinking intensively about what typography is today. in some cases investigations of this kind have taken on the scale of books, some of which were even published. there was a book about cars, one about cooking and one about typography.

we have been working for ERCO for over a decade. in our own judgement the result reflects the fact that it too is a middle-sized company, a family firm with a management for whom design and form have even become the crucial economic motivation. the company earns its money with its immense activities for design and uses design not as decoration and an attractive covering. the form of the products is identical with their technical function. or is intended to become so. there is no end to this if high standards of making form and technology identical are set.

the company and its circle of partners is so manageable
that it is possible to hold a conversation where otherwise
instructions are issued.

the classic allocation of authority is abolished. entre-
peneurs, engineers, product designers, architects and
graphic designers sit down at the same table, this is not
to be understood in terms of simultaneity, although the
circle often is quite large, but in the sense of inner
involvement. every subject affects everybody, even if
responsibilities are different. the crucial thing is not
departmental authority, but better arguments, better suggestions, better reasons.

the highest court of appeal, taken quite literally, the
highest institution in the entire factory complex, only to
be reached by a flight of winding stairs, is a round table.
this round table is older than the one invented by the
poles. not even the entrepreneur has status authority, he
owes his position to his argument and his ability to evaluate. it corresponds with the passion with which he
approaches the matter in hand.

i know german industry, its managers. there are worlds
of difference in the kinds of leadership one finds. for me,
as far as the result of my work and my working methods
are concerned, the key is that i am only as good as my
partners.

the munich olympics would never have been what
they were, despite terrorist activity and blood baths, if
there had not been an extraordinary president of the
organizing committee. i never expected him to tell me
what means would be available for our use. that was
our affair. but we defined what the aim of the whole
thing was in constant dialogue, going to the stage of
formulating concepts and theses about what general
intentions should be developed, what projected image
was to be striven for and what experience content we
should communicate. sporting facts, said willi daume,
are soon forgotten. the experience is what counts.
expressed in my philosophy: the olympic games are an
analoguous, not a digital event. you take away with you
what you see and what is determined by your own
evaluation, the form of the experience. the figures you
forget. we quoted ludwig wittgenstein and william of
ockham to make it clear that reality is a communicative
achievement.

it is no longer valid to say: here is reality, here are
things, here is technology and there are words, images
merely as copy-images. things exist, and are there in
their appearance itself.

thus choosing colours for this colourful event was not a question of taste or following a trend, but a question of argument. we could say precisely why the colour range should look like this and no different. we had developed a philosophy. translating this into concrete designs was a thing in itself, but it was not thinkable without a comprehensive working hypothesis and a comprehensive programme.

but here too it is true that: huge though the event was, the team that realized it was very small. it was a manageable enterprise, somewhat patched together and perhaps not as closely knit as in a company like ERCO.

klaus jürgen maack was asked what he thought about corporate identity. not a lot, nothing, he said. and he knows what he is talking about. he doesn't say it critically because he has objections to dressing-up methods, but from the experience of an approach that has been put into practice.

in the case of an enterprise in which there is so much thinking and considering, sketching, developing and rejecting, i ask what colour could stand for this enterprise. and i ask my colleagues in discussion if they dream in colour or in black and white, whether they think in colour or black and white. the nature of light also leads me to a contrast of black and white, of light source and shade, of bright and dark.

in the colour climate of the enterprise we agree on a scale of grey, between black and white. this too, although white light is the source of all colours we perceive, through the refraction of rays of light. occasionally we also allow colour to carry some weight.

in another case, where we had also agreed on a grey series, for an insurance company, we cut out colour altogether, not even colour photography was used which in the case of the olympic games for instance was the only form of pictorial representation we permitted, something absolutely new, and not just that, but highly demanding. since then all tourist office prospectuses have been in colour. meanwhile we enjoy the clear winter landscape and intelligence landscape of science and technology. intelligence and morality are colourless.

i have invented a few colours in my lifetime. of course i did not invent them as such. all the colours that we see are there. but we see only those colours that we have in our consciousness, that we can name. we see only that which we know and can name communicatively as an object of information. the colour turquoise has existed only since the empire. it was not known in the middle ages, even though matthias grünewald almost achieved turquoise in the halo of the risen christ.

in the field of grey we have invented two colours. one went into the language of colour as greige, and is used in department stores for things like describing the colour of women's stockings. it is a mixture of grey and sand colour. there are countless colour shades in the field of grey, more than among the bright colours. you can get enthusiastic about it, and you do not have to be afraid of disrespectful bleak and dreary grey. the other grey is called vlau. the word has not yet become established. i am certain that it will come, as this colour is the most exciting colour in the late twentieth century. recently i wanted to see a high-rise office block in tokyo in this colour. but the american firm supplying the cladding could not manufacture it.

both these shades of grey played a part in the visual image of ERCO. the company sees light and lighting in strict relation to modern architecture, to the lighting of spaces in general. this was originally an architecture of classical modernism from mies van der rohe down to harry seidler, who is still working, or the representatives of a formal, geometrical design concept. mies van der rohe was very interested in radiation from his architecture, at night as well. he did not simply install light, but had walls or floors illuminated as light areas.

a shade of brown was appropriate to his world of travertine and bronze, in the seagram building for example. in the early stages of our work with ERCO we preferred a brownish grey, our greige. this was used in places where we needed a general background for pictorial accounts, for photographs or drawings of products.

this grey has died out in the meantime. perhaps this has struck no-one outside. but we are entirely convinced that this would be the wrong colour for a firm like ERCO today.

architecture, if one ignores its occasional fashionable appearances when everything is pink or sky-blue, is nowadays much more speculative, constructive, technical, rational, functional than the art architecture of simplicity and aesthetic reduction of circle, square and triangle. piet mondrian is no longer a stimulus for architecture. it is more likely to be a crane, a suspension bridge, an engine. today architecture, at least we hope, is thought out, designed, constructed, not felt first, or related to historical aesthetic models.

this means that we have to alter our scale of grey, from greige to vlau, from feeling to thinking.

vlau is a combination of violet and grey. blue and violet are a spiritual realm. the sky is blue. twilight is blueish like longing and dreams in perspective, beethoven writes music in full colour, mozart in tones, and often in a grey-blue mood. the grey we mean is not neutral. it is electrified.

so now ERCO has a different scale of grey, arising from an effort to bring form and process into line. the firm has changed. the relationship of light and architecture is different. architecture exists at night and during the day through light. there is no dark architecture.

what light and what lamps does contemporary architecture need? that is a problem that ultimately leads to the decision that we now have to use vlau rather than greige. and it is by no means out of the question that in looking for an adequate correspondence of wanting and obligation we will invent a new grey. for the time being we are content with vlau and see our attitude confirmed over a large area.

in a similar way we are constantly thinking about everything. the logogram is a simple aesthetic phenomenon. a simple response to a major, complex demand. we wanted to translate light into typography. and to a certain extent in real terms, not symbolically.

a symbolic solution would have been to look for something representing a kind of light source, a lamp, the sun, as many people do who have to find an image for a lighting firm. no, we wanted light as a structure, and we wanted light in its manifestation as typography, in the sequence of letters. we wanted to recreate the medium in its communicative form, light as a typeface.

in specialist jargon one would say: we were looking for a syntactic, not a semantic solution. syntactic means looking for structural affinity rather than a symbolic pictorial comparison dragged in by the scruff of its neck.

neither dürer's praying hands nor heaven-storming gothic architecture is a symbol of religion. kierkegaard would have been more likely to choose a symbol of loneliness.

we think that the ERCO logo is a clear statement. we can see no reason to question it, simple though it is. in design one should not be afraid of the simplest solutions, if they fit the bill. only ornament and decoration are excessive. the most important example of an emblem for graphic designers is the red dot on a white field that is the sign for japan. there is nothing to be taken away, nothing to be added, even though it could not possibly be simpler.

here we are moving in the realm of signs and sign functions. but language does not consist of words, but of
sentences, the proposition is the smallest unit of thought.
you have to put together a correlation of at least two
elements to be able to make a statement, a single word
is dumb. the world consists of states of affairs, they are
represented in propositions, in sentences.

and a company does not just wish to show itself, it
wants to speak. it wants to articulate itself. above all, if
it does not just sell products that exist as such, but
products that do something, achieve something, are used
as part of processes, have dynamic status. if one is trying
to provide space for a company that wants to put itself
over, to articulate itself, then it is not enough to make
only words available, only to develop signs. one has to
create a linguistic form, the visual and verbal language of
the company.

and it is also not enough for verbal expression to think
only about proper language. in the field of visual language we are moving in undiscovered territories. what is
the sign language of a company like? here we feel like
adam in paradise, giving names to things.

the company provides information about products,
about their use, their components, their equipment, their
effect, about the reliability of their effect, about expense
and use, about application limitations, about side effects,
about consumption of energy and ultimately about price
and cost.

how does one say that?

thinking about this leads to an independent corporate
language. it is as individual and autonomous as aramaic
compared to turkish. fortunately, visual languages are
more internationally comprehensible than verbal languages, which means that images gain priority over
words, in complete contrast with our modern information
culture.

this language presents itself in different media. ERCO
even has a house magazine that appears periodically. this
language presents itself in various layouts. the layout for
a report is different from that of a catalogue, and this
language presents itself in a certain kind of photography,
a certain philosophy of pictorial representation. only a
limited number of photographers have access to the
company.

four criteria for the selection of photographs:
– it should not be possible to tell that a photograph is
posed, structured or manipulated. it can only be credible
if the photographer withdraws from the picture.

- a photograph should not try to be a work of art, and so not appear as an end in itself. what counts is the approach to the matter to be presented.
- a photograph may not alienate. photography is communication. it must make itself precise, by capturing the moment.
- a photograph is a representation of states of affairs. it must show a thing in its behaviour. it must catch processes, procedures, developments, evolution.

these premises do not sound particularly demanding. however there are only a few photographers who meet them. making something that should be taken completely for granted is here again turned into art. in this way our world has taken on such remarkable traits that it becomes difficult to get hold of a good bottle of wine or good black bread. or a good picture.

most photographs are forced, ambitious, show off, strike attitudes, make themselves beautiful.

developing a visual language is a complex process, and discussion about it has not yet been concluded within the firm. we are fairly sure how statements about a particular product have to look, but we are open in the question of how a product should appear in advertising, in public. opinions differ. but insights develop from the articulation of various points of view and assessments.

and this is not a struggle for position, it is a discussion about questions to which there is not yet an answer. a company can be in the front line of cultural development as well, for instance as far as the question of the visual languages to be developed in order to convey what cannot be said in words is concerned. the main thing is to avoid false overtones. the man responsible for visual language at ERCO is from the ruhr, and can tell when any of his mates is pushing, showing off or shooting a line.

our office has provenly done a great deal to develop new visual languages. the pictograms at frankfurt airport and for the olympic games have become an international sign language that is now taken for granted. a few decades ago it did not exist. information had to be acquired mainly through reading.

these can only be indications of the terrain into which one is moving if a company is trying to agree on what should happen and how it might look, what has to be said and the question of how it comes over.

but the visual appearance of a company cannot avoid the question of the internal impression it makes. usually all that people look at is the external impression.

164

perhaps nobody will believe it, but it is a fact: all ERCO's machine tools have been or are being repainted. a new world of work has come into being. away from the factory and moving towards the laboratory. away from force, on towards intelligence.

the company does not provide striking solutions for light sources, beautiful lamps, something like technical suns or technical monstrances, but intelligent solutions for lighting requirements. and so the employees have to work in an environment of intelligent stimulation as well. ERCO's workrooms no longer belong to the old factory, not even to the beautifully colourful one in which people were said to like working so much.

this also leads to the question of harmony of architecture, the firm's own buildings, with company culture. the ERCO factories date from various periods and company concepts. every time a new building was needed the question recurred: what should it look like?

of course you can call in an architect and ask him to provide his own best solution, analogous with his reputation and methods, to capture the spirit of the age. this will not do for ERCO. the question is: what appearance is appropriate to the company culture at this moment, what appearance is appropriate to the design concept, the communication culture? architecture is part of visual appearance.

and so the most diverse people discuss criteria for appropriate selfrepresentation in buildings at the round table at the highest point of the company, possible architects are selected, they are asked to present their thoughts and they are confronted with the programme for both the building task and the appearance of the building. the chairman formulates some premises, explains the expected attitude. in the most recent case he thought of the formulation that his building should be an "overall for a technical centre". this is an attractive and appealing formulation from the company's point of view, which is even suitable to fertilize contemporary architectural theory, which has more to do with suits and pin-stripes. in the mean time, with building work concluded, the architect too has become a friend of the family, not just the receiver of the commission to whom the company has said thank you. he has been seen as someone who thinks with them, thinks in terms of company scale: what architecture is appropriate to the status of the firm?

conventional consideration of the concept of corporate identity would now ask about graphic elements like lettering and typography. this can be ignored here, as even a typeface is not the application of the latest fashion. it is a considerable subject in its own right for thought outside matters of design fashion. in the mean time the problem has been so thoroughly worked over that new typefaces have been developed because type as well could be a manifestation of an advanced design position. this is in flux. perhaps ERCO will appear with a new house typeface tomorrow.

design is the life procedure of a company if intentions are to be concretized into facts and phenomena. intentions are to become appearance. this needs technical provision, but also the form in which this will appear.

design is the substance of the company alongside the bare economy of numbers. it is not a little coat. it is the centre of company culture, of innovative and creative concern with the purpose of the company.

the workshop in which this is achieved is also the medium from which company philosophy grows. it was a bold stroke to arrive at the formula: "we don't make lamps, we make better light". this means that if so far lighting firms have made beautiful lamps, from the chandelier to the tulip lamp or spots styled in a modern way à la hollein or sottsass, ERCO claims to manufacture lamps that fulfil lighting tasks, not just as a made up technical product but in terms of a technical aspiration that would not even have to be afraid of the emperor of japan's reception room.

better light, not lamps. or lamps for better light. that is a company concept. it would also be, appropriately reformulated, a concept for industrial production overall. it is not the product that counts, it is its performance, its development, its use. and the product should not be an end in itself in terms of appearance, but the picture of its task. finding this is a piece of culture.

the modern designer's dream is to make a car. but are cars thought of as objects that evolve from their purpose? as elements in a traffic system? they are still highly-styled prestige demonstrations that are evaluated outside their function in the present traffic network. they are dreams. their appearance is not the appearance of their self, because this would be the appearance of their task. they are symbols. to hell with symbols. back to things.

the word symbol may be eradicated from our vocabulary. art may turn to the symbol. a more humane world with the range of intelligence that we have to offer has to abide with the things.

166

graphic designers' space to be themselves

graphic design is one of the last free professions that is not forced into the corset of a career structure and thus inhibited by standards and guidelines. there is no career structure upon which the state could accompany designers with examinations and checks, and of course also with certificates and prizes, with awards and titles. a graphic designer is a graphic designer. he is what he can.

even for architects this is different. an architect does not just want to build well, he wants to become chief architect, district architect, government architect or professor. and he can only achieve that if the state says how architecture is to be seen as a profession.

today the profession of architect as such is protected, only those bearing the title architect are permitted to build. and this title is bestowed by the state. twenty years ago anyone could build his house himself. he had to prove that it complied with building regulations and wouldn't fall down. at that time i was allowed to draw the rotis buildings myself. the district master builder approved them without any fuss. recently, when i had to enlarge one of the buildings, in the same style as the one in which they are built, i had to use an architect and the planning application went through town and district to government level. the whole thing was turned down, went through all the levels of appeal again and was finally passed, having taken a year in the process.

graphic designers are graphic designers as a result of their abilities. graphic designers have no titles, just as writers or rock-stars don't. there are no junior writers and chief writers, no doctors of writing, and a professor of writing is, at least so far, preposterous.

the converse is more like the case: anyone who wanted to quote any title, on a letter-head, a business card, the title page of a book or a front door would not be taken seriously. he would be suspected of needing to put rank before ability. even thomas mann, who paid some heed to rank and name, just had plain thomas mann on his front door.

classification of a writer by the state still seems to us to be a mockery of cultural freedom. a writer with a state title would be a ridiculous figure. but let us be careful: the state has already reached the point of influencing the classification of literature, with honorific titles as a first step. and there could be the one or the other writer who would allow himself to be declared chief or government writer within the framework of state hierarchization in the form of a career structure, because then all his financial problems would be solved. he could become a civil servant.

in music the interconnection of profession and state is very much closer than in architecture. who is still a free-lance musician? the piano teacher round the corner, just.

why should this be out of the question in literature? there would then be salary scales that could be calculated accurately, as for district architects, city architects and government architects or professors. why must writers, the minister of culture would say, write on the minimum necessary for existence, driving themselves to the verge of suicide like rilke, musil or trakl?

in the mean time it has gradually become a custom that authors no longer print just their names in their books, but their titles as well. friedrich schiller was professor of history, but he would have made himself a laughing stock if he had presented his *maria stuart* under the name of "professor friedrich schiller". he would not even have been able to permit himself a hint at an academic teaching activity without arousing the suspicion that as a free-lance poet he was in someone's service as well. (which he really was, look at his development from *die räuber* to *wallenstein*.)

painters as well, artist painters, as far as their letterheads are concerned, no longer present themselves by name, but under their full title. but what would professor michelangelo or professor picasso mean for us. le corbusier refused the title of professor because he must have sensed that his antiacademic architecture, his architecture of free personal design would thus have had the blessing of officialdom and would have become second rate, in fact academic. in these fields titles reduce the dignity of autonomous making and the independence of creative drives.

certainly it is not a particular merit of graphic designers if they do not yet have a career structure made official by the state and so do not have certificates and titles. probably they have simply been forgotten so far. and a lot of people are already working on changing things. another reason to drink deeply of the freedom one is given if one works only in one's own name.

however, it is not just a question of cultural dignity, namely to do his work as a free, independent, non-dependent, non-organized person without ties, following only his own criteria of thinking and feeling, it is also a question of efficiency.

my doctor, to whom i have been loyal for many years, recently made a bitter complaint about the undermining of his profession. he is a respected man in a hospital. formerly, he said, he had been able to devote himself entirely to his patients. he was able to see illness as a problem for people, of individual fates. today half of his professional life is taken up with proving that he is measuring up to standards and guidelines, he is a slave to a constant flow of new directives and has perpetually to be reading his way into the language of new forms. as a respected doctor he has to permit employees of a medical insurance scheme to tell him that he has to fill some forms in again because he hadn't done it correctly. my profession is dead, he says. i have advised none of my children to become a doctor. medicine has become a perfect system of standards and conditions, performance and assessment, transformations and translations, a supermachine in which the doctor, who was once the crown of medicine, is only a very small cog. certainly he still has some latitude, but that is used for conforming, not for creativity, initiative and problem solving.

this says two things. one is that, seen quite superficially, one has less time for the thing for which one is there. and the second is that the quality of the actual work has changed. one is no longer a free doctor, but someone who is observed, about whom checks are made.

and this is not a phenomenon only in the state health service, it is not very different in the universities, and anyone who knows his way around largescale, centrally managed commercial organizations can tell you a thing or two about where bureaucracy can lead.

graphic designers are still free. they live in the free air of real ability. the stimulus of their work comes from what they do themselves. even a master painter, a decorator has training standards, is obliged to prove performance, has to document the stages of his professional development with examinations and official proofs of performance, which incidentally necessarily makes the examiners appointed as organs of state administration seem far more important than the decorator himself.

it is possible that the painting trade would flourish of its own accord, without organs of state supervision. in the mean time pretty well everyone can paper or paint his own room. but where would that leave the officials? where would be the claim of the modern state to order everything by regulation, down to our awareness of history?

graphic designers are still not hemmed in by forms, books of standards, job descriptions and the appropriate regulatory personnel. at the moment they do not have to belong to a professional organization, not yet.

anyone can call himself a graphic designer. our profession is open to anyone. this is almost an uplifting feeling. where can you still find that?

but the state already wants to know if you are a qualified graphic designer if for instance you try to get yourself classified as a free lance for tax purposes. and this is where the problems start. the state does not believe that you are a graphic designer if you say yourself that you are. it goes without saying that it has no idea what a graphic designer is and also does not want to have an idea. it could only believe it if you had passed an official examination or can produce some official confirmation. if you present the official with books in which people write about your work as a graphic designer they do not accept that. the state does not want to understand, it wants to be correct in evaluating its regulations. and where there are no regulations you cannot form a judgement about the way they have been interpreted.

fortunately the state too has recently also appointed professors who teach what graphic design might possibly be. when they pronounce a judgement for an authority it is just accepted, usually in association with the remark that this is more or less a subjective judgement. so where is the state-attested career structure? and indeed not only the state has an interest in there at last being guidelines for graphic designers as well. even professional organizations and associations promise themselves enhanced value if they are allowed a say who is and who isn't a graphic designer. and of course there would then be professional ranks and professional titles to satisfy that most human of weaknesses that no-one could possibly condemn, and that is vanity. and then, after a system of this kind has been introduced, it will be possible, like government architects, to rest more or less from a certain stage, because you don't have to keep on having ideas as you reach a ripe old age.

but, at the moment anyway, you don't even need to have been at a state school as a graphic designer. a graphic designer is someone who can translate the world and what happens in it into signs and pictures, who can make visible what is not visible. this is a high cultural activity. it is possible to assess its status if you follow how ludwig wittgenstein for instance placed the distinction between "sagen" (say) and "zeigen" (show) at the centre of his philosophy. The word "zeigen" contains the word "zeichen" (sign). and graphic designers are concerned in a concrete way with the difference between saying and showing, between digital and analoguous information.

is it not a wonderful state of affairs that, in order to work at the centre of modern cultural problems you do not even have to have attended a state college? what can one say, what can one show?

in rotis there are graphic designers who have enjoyed graphic training in a college, alongside those who have learned only writing and arithmetic we also know that schools can be a great help. but not necessarily. on the contrary: they can also destroy.

being a graphic designer is indeed a rare privilege. who is still as free and has so few ties that he can develop the whole of his profession out of himself? in order to reach this right royal condition one must of course not step into the traps that the state has laid in order to make this profession as well conform with its official guidelines.

we are hurrying with rapid steps into a new form of the total state, which regulates the entire lives of its citizens like a deus ex machina. it is this kind of leadership that is made possible by computer technology, total intelligibility of the world around us from a centre. the paths to this state are not called compulsion and dominance, but title and income.

the traps that are set for all who can still take off under their own steam, are delicate, but effective. who wants to withdraw from state honours?

the state distributes honours, professorships, honorary doctorates. who would want to see that as a trap? who would not like to be a professor?

the sociology of honours is not always seen through. the joy of public recognition, satisfaction of vanity are so dominant that one can hardly spare a glance for real intentions and the mechanism of effects.

why does the state need heroes? because otherwise it can no longer fight wars. an individual soldier gains nothing if his country conquers new territory. he goes home after the war, does his work. war as such gives him nothing. but if he brings home a decoration . . .

but how do you make heroes? by giving them honours. but how? with a decoration, a little piece of secular tin, with a certificate, a handshake, above all with a public citation, with promotions and titles. all things that don't cost anything.

many a soldier has behaved bravely without consideration of his life, sacrificed himself for his comrades and his unit. but he only remains in the best memory of those who know his story if he is accepted into the circle of those who allot a higher meaning to war, into the circle of heroes of the fatherland. the honour and dignity arising from it are something of the highest that a person can acquire, the ceremonial expenditure is nothing. it costs the state nothing to make heroes, but it gains the readiness of others to become heroes as well. it gains people for the ends of its war. there would probably soon be no wars any more if states rewarded their heroes in material terms, a pension for life, for instance, corresponding to the intended honour.

and the state certainly awards professorships from the ministry of culture partly to honour achievement. but if you look more closely at who recovers this kind of honour you will be surprised how much method there can be in the distribution of honours. often the person giving the honour distinguishes himself more than the person honoured, and then every person honoured becomes more obliging as far as the person who has honoured him is concerned. the state would be a mere purpose-orientated administration like the postal service if it had not taken upon itself the right to distribute titles and honours. in this way it becomes a dignity, an authority that sets values.

the state has also crept into the guild of graphic designers with titles and honours. clearly the present state does not like it if people do something they want themselves. everything is supposed to serve the public good. the prerequisite here is that there is only one court of appeal that can say what the public good is. to this extent the state would like to say what is right for all professions, and for graphic designers as well.

we graphic designers are still fair game socially. we don't fence ourselves off. and we enjoy that. we find out by our own means what graphic design is, and try to work out for ourselves the direction in which it can develop. this autonomy of making is like mountain air. it is probably even a prerequisite of real creativity, of creativity that is sensed as natural growth with a passion for our own, undirected developments. and this freedom of doing is seen as a prerequisite for gaining one's own certainty and self-trust, elementary prerequisites of being able to do things.

it can be proved that designers, when they take over an academic activity and are thus bound into modern adminstrative pedagogy, begin to flag in their creative achievements. the concept "civil servant" is synonymous with noncreative behaviour, with burnt-out fire. even fear of critical students forces conformity.

freedom is stimulating. it is not just that an enormous amount of time and energy is absorbed in sustaining the apparatus in administered academies and colleges. there is also a lack of administrative scope which stands in the way of imagination and uninhibited design.

we know that our freedom is in jeopardy. and so it is also recommended that no-one joins any of the professional associations, who in their way want to present proof of their right to exist. normally one pays contributions for secretaries and a board. the money is usually not sufficient for more than self-representation of these organs, perhaps just for the free participation of these organs in congresses at which the other members have to pay for the pleasure of seeing someone again out of their own pockets. such associations enjoy the favour of the state and like to join in with making graphic design an official profession. such associations often came into being as a result of high joint cultural aims. but they too need money. and alongside awards and honours the state has another seductive method for drawing everything to itself: from the taxes that we pay to it, it pays subsidies as the fancy takes it. and what association, what institute, is still working without state subsidy today?

we in rotis guard our freedom like the apple of our eye and have developed a sixth sense for checking whether declarations of love are not lime-twigs to tie us into the dirigisme of the modern state. our little institute does not accept professorships or state funds.

we are not saying that we have to do with a wicked state, outside any qualification the state as state is an evil if it interferes with free spaces where creativity means as much as undisturbed and uncontrolled making. once on the same morning two offers of appointment to illustrious professorships came in. it is good to live in a working atmosphere where such impudent requests can be wafted away like paper in the light of dawn.

recently a light aircraft flew once round the earth without refuelling. the three people who developed and built this aircraft over four years also declined all state subsidy. they found the money themselves. that shows spirit. it is intellectual sportsmanship.

we decisively, determinedly, unyieldingly reject any state authority as far as graphic design is concerned.

every one of us knows more than it does, every one. it is an abstruse idea that the state might have anything to do with our work. and as the state loves only those that it can embrace, we reject any acts of kindness.

this has disadvantages.

the master decorator of whom we spoke is allowed to train apprentices. it has been confirmed that he works along lines laid down by the state, we do not have any such guidelines and confirmations. and so we are not allowed to train. this state is as perfect as that. on the one hand it offers us the federal cross of merit first class for just a single one of our projects. on the other hand we are not allowed to train anyone. of course with the exception of those who can afford to go without proofs of achievement. and who can do that today? people who rely on themselves. and they are not the worst.

a new typeface

why do we need a new typeface? this question is justified. with the replacement of hot metal printing by pho-
tosetting the number of typefaces has increased by leaps
and bounds. it is an easy matter to put any number of
typefaces into a data base and then expose the individual
letters on photographic paper or film. and photographic
or film material is sufficient for most printing processes
today.

so why increase this typeface inflation by yet another
face? typeface asceticism, limitation of diversity should
be what is demanded.

on the other hand typefaces can also be seen from the
point of view of whether the development of type is finished, has come to a standstill today. whether one
should, as is said in architecture, withdraw to quotations.
typefaces can be seen from the point of view of their
use, the optimization of their reading quality, instead of,
as usually happens today, that of their formal quality,
their aesthetic satisfaction.

if one thinks like this and gives priority to the quality
of use it is certainly easy to come to the conclusion that
most modern faces are nonsensical because they are not
suitable for printing a novel. it would be too difficult to
read, one would be too quick to put the book down. and
at the same time you would come to the conclusion that
even good typefaces cannot be the last word. their quality is not adequate any more.

to find that out one needs a precise definition of the
assessment criteria.

faces have to be analysed, they have to be tested in
use.

the belief is long past that typefaces are good if they
are built up on formal basic elements like circle, square
or triangle. that was the way the bauhaus thought, and
this basic principle is still dominant in renner's "futura".
all one has to do is make the attempt to reshape one's
own handwriting on this principle. and handwriting, as a
used script, is still an outstanding testbed for finding out
what makes typefaces good or bad. it is a good idea to
abandon any formal code if one wants to test what a
typeface is worth.

one should not overtax the old masters either. people
of the calibre of claude garamond or giambattista bodoni
were not concerned with optimizing legibility, simply
because that was not a question at the time. they

e

abcdefgh
ijklmnopqr
stuvw
xyz

semigrotesk
semigrotesk
semigrotesk

antiqua abcdefgh
ijklmnopqr
stuvw
xyz

grotesk abcdefgh
ijklmnopqr
stuvw
xyz

otl aicher, "rotis" type
family in grotesque,
semi-grotesque
and roman, 1988.

unquestioningly possessed a feeling for a manageable face, they did not think much of analytical criteria. at that time people read folios, not paperbacks.

the development of typefaces is more interesting in the context of the development of great newspapers. even in the 19th century many faces were drawn and cut to meet the demand of accommodating the maximum of text in the minimum of space without affecting legibility. one of the best modern faces, "times", came into being as a result of a newspaper commission. it would be worth working through this epoch of typeface development, which has remained a stepchild of a more artistic way of looking at things. it produced as much for typography as the iron structures of engineering architecture for the development of new building.

it is not the beautiful book but the daily paper, not beautiful calligraphy but everyday handwriting that are the testing ground of reading and writing, and thus release the crucial criteria of evaluation. and if you are in a situation to ask the right questions you are also close to the right solution. there is no way of avoiding thinking. you will not get very far with typefaces with an aversion to rationalism.

developing a new typeface in the sense of a further development begins with the setting up of an evaluation catalogue. it begins with the question of what is to be asked.

we no longer read as we used to. we lack time and leisure. additionally we have seen that visual media often inform more quickly and comprehensively than verbal ones. there is a growing number of people who never pick up a book, but instead acquire their insights from the television. is there a typeface that can be read more easily and more rapidly than the existing ones? how can one increase recognizability, legibility, reading speed?

to answer these questions the printing firm of maack in lüdenscheid has set up a studio in rotis to pursue these and related questions. modern electronic techniques cannot design themselves, but they are particularly suited to modifying faces that are fed into them. thinking is the investigation of differences. so it is better to think about typefaces if one quickly has the modifications of a typeface to hand. for this purpose a computer with a plotter is good either as a setting apparatus or as a special device for electronically controlled typeface development.

it is a relatively long process to feed the co-ordinates of a letter along its contours into a computer. but then it is easy for the computer to make it thicker or thinner, more slender or broader, to place it straight or obliquely, to make it larger or smaller.

but this does not allow you to get away from the fact that before this every letter has to be drawn by hand before it is digitalized in the computer. designing it is an analoguous procedure, finishing a digital one.

plotters are drawing geniuses. in seconds they draws the outline of a letter on paper or cut it two-dimensionally out of plastic foil with a high-grade knife. it does this with the highest degree of accuracy, although only the larger letter sizes. letter shapes in reading size are achieved by reduction in reproduction. and it is only in reading size that a letter reveals its qualities in the context of other letters. we do not read letters, but word pictures. in this way something comes into the design of a typeface that one cannot draw at all: distance apart, free space.

determining the distance between letters is of great importance as far as reading quality is concerned. to this extent the person who says that designing a typeface is a matter of getting the black and the white into the right balance is on the right lines. the positive is defined by the negative, the negative by the positive. black and white have the same meaning.

the computer is called fritz. we have known him for a long time. first he helped monika schnell to draw structures for gift wrapping paper. now she can pursue her former activity of working with barbara klein on drawing typefaces, giving the right balance to black and white.

the world as design

the world can be seen as a constantly predetermined cosmos, a given condition into which we are bound. this is how the ancients saw it, both in their idealistic and realistic schools. this is how the christian middle ages saw it, and the british empiricists as well.

the world can be understood as a process of development into which one is born. then a static model is replaced by a kinetic one. this is how we have learned to see the world since lamarck and darwin, and how we like to see it today under the influence of behaviourism and behavioural research.

and the world can be seen as a design.

as a design, that is to say as a product of a civilization, as a world made and organized by men. then it is, even in the case of predetermined nature, a world of designs and also bad designs, and nature becomes part of this world and has to fall into line with it.

for goethe the world was still one of nature and history, and the philosopher from königsberg would admit only two domains of philosophy: the domain of nature and the domain of freedom.

if you open a newspaper today it is full of talk about cars and rockets, aeroplanes and transit tunnels, factories and production lines, perfumes and harmful chemicals, football stadiums and multi-storey car parks, clothes and clinics, satellites and mountain bikes, nouvelle cuisine and rubbish mountains, atom bombs and museums, festivals and wars, butter mountains and film premières, groundwater contamination and fashion shows, cfcs and ozone, artificial ice and rat poison.

the world in which we live is the world we made. everyone was shocked when darwin explained that man descended from monkeys. but that was more the shock of saying that men and monkeys were equal. and indeed it is possible to take offence at that. darwin suffered from condemnation of a formulation that he did not make in that way. in reality darwin came to conclusions that were far more provocative but which did not give offence. darwin reversed the entire principle of explaining the world as it came down to us through the ancients, christianity and the west.

as far as he was concerned there was no longer a plan in the world, no law of cause and effect in the sense of causal drives, no spiritual principle to guide and control, no god as creator, no spirit that rules the world. there was no longer any point in looking for causes for particular effects, the effects themselves are the cause of world development. what confirmed itself in practice is the selective principle of forms of appearance. no reason of any kind controls the development of the world, its way is determined by the selective principle of effect, of effectivity. just as everything arranges itself in the interplay with other things.

nature is not logical, it is not determined. nature plays and leaves what is to survive to proving in life, to the fact, to the effect.

how does nature play? you do not need to make the effort of wanting to understand the principle of mutation in order to recognize the game character of nature. it can be seen in the very fact that almost all living beings exist in two sexes. precisely speaking the human being as a human being does not exist, it only exists as man and woman. sexuality is the methodical basis by which the world does not constantly repeat itself, constantly reiterate, but changes and develops. reproduction of man and woman always produces man and woman, but in the greatest possible variety. the prerequisite for the development of nature is variation. variations require a world with two poles. variants mediate progress by being exposed to proving themselves in life, and what is better survives. development is based on dissolution of being into two elements.

in philosophy, in understanding the world, people have always looked for the great unit, the being. but the world of units is a monumental world, it is frozen into a single condition. it is not until there is interconnection, the dissolution of units, and also through death, that the world becomes creative. it develops models that constantly bring about new variations and new constellations. the world plays and leaves decisions about victory and defeat to the judgement of the factual, of effect. what is left over is called expedient.

even today we are still hardly aware what a reversal that means. law, order, planning, reason, previously seen as the basis of the world, are questioned. and thus also the thing we call spirit. legalities and principles of order are not fundamentally rejected, but tolerated only in the same way that one can discover the thread running through a person's biography only when his life is over. even in the last year of his life he can do something that gives a new meaning to that life. it is only in retrospect that consistency can be perceived, but we should not define this as purposefulness, but as a result.

even mathematics, the most logical of all sciences, was shaken in its belief in logical consequence. alan turing addressed david hilbert's, kurt gödel's and john von neumann's problem of how mathematics could be proved in its correctness and competence in the abstract, by logical conclusions and evidence. he did not produce his proof through a new chain of logical reasoning, but by the working method of a machine that could operate mathematically, i.e. carry out processes and achieve effects. this calculating machine became our computer. the effect explains the law.

that was pretty much the end of mathematics as theory. mathematical assumptions cannot be proved conclusively, their correctness cannot be definitively grounded in logic. today, mathematics are created and confirmed by computer. this is not the end of mathematics, but the end of a kind of mathematics that justifies itself by consequential logic, by compelling conclusions.

quantum mechanics had already given a hint of this development. we cannot say what form an elementary particle has, whether it is a corpuscle or a wave, and at the same time state the place where it is to be found. determinism is statistical. it occurs, but it cannot be defined. it can be detected, but not predicted.

if there is a reason for the world, it is that of its functionality. this shows in the way in which purposes are fulfilled.

ever since men have existed they have perceived themselves as part of the cosmos. they have defined themselves from the explanation of the world. the philosophical tool of this self-definition was epistemology. what is the world for human beings, how do they acquire it, what is their bond with it?

how is cognition possible? this was an attempt to answer how we are linked to the world. cognition was the bond between subject and object.

the traditional understanding of cognition was that it was the representation of the world in us. as painting creates pictures, so reason creates copies of what exists.

but for a long time there has been painting without copies, and, just as there is constructivist painting there is a constructivist theory of cognition. it leads to the conclusion that human cognition is self-effected, a technique of forming concepts and definitions that at best yields a model of the world, but not a copy. the mind as a combining substance between world and human being, as a medium of participation, is increasingly seen as intellect, as an instrument for the production of information. mind is reduced to information and the processing of it.

fifty years ago a philosophy of technology hardly existed. today we no longer perceive man as a natural creature drawing his strength from being, but as the maker of an autonomous technology that can on the one hand fly to the moon but on the other hand is in a position to extinguish life on earth, by means of either nuclear physics or chemistry.

we are becoming aware that man, whether for good or bad, has stepped outside nature. he is bound to it, but he builds a second world over it, that of his own constructions. our world is no longer nature embedded in the cosmos. in a pubertal rush of self-decision we have detached ourselves from alliance with universals and follow our own ends. these turn out to be as daredevil as they are fatal and we would have to accept it if, because of our constructive autonomy, mankind were to cease to exist in the next century. humanity still has no morality of technical, scientific, economic development. perhaps because we were not intellectually prepared for such a powerful termination of old connections and old truths.

to this day man's new situation is acquired less by insights than by fear of an autonomy that possibly can no longer be controlled, which is at the same time hectic, blind and also breathtaking. we continue to philosophize about the world as "being" and overlook the fact that it has become a design, a fabricated model, that even includes nature.

even immanuel kant introduced "one additional principle" into philosophy that did not rest on causal conclusions. it is a reflective principle. in contrast with reason and understanding he called it "urteilskraft" (power of judgment). the "reflective power of judgement" does not wish to find the cause of things, but their purpose, what they are good for. he moves from a causal explanation to a teleological one. things are no longer determined by a principle of reason, but by their purposiveness. for nature, this is their viability. with "reflective power of judgement" and the "imagination" associated with it we think of the world from the point of view of the concrete, the special, and no longer on general principles.

something is purposive if it is in agreement with itself. for kant that criterion of purposiveness is not use, but an idea towards which something is directed, its finality. it was not until the next century that efficiency itself became the measure of purposiveness. this happened in the natural sciences. and it was not until the

20th century that use (gebrauch) was raised to the status of being a central concept, even in philosophy. (today though it seems to have been replaced by "consumption" [verbrauch]).

the mathematician hilbert also doubted whether it was true that two times two equals four. he doubted whether the laws of mathematics permitted conclusions concerning the laws of reality. but it is beyond dispute that it was the enormous explanatory culture of mathematics and the sciences that made a great brain out of the earth, a great traffic network everywhere, an industrial landscape and a single market of products, information and services.

the discipline of thinking occasioned by logic and algebra, the expansion of thinking space through formulae and abstract algorithms has caused the emergence of structures that reduce the existing planet to an agricultural plant. and between building sites and rubbish dumps we enjoy hitherto unknown leisure time and freedom of consumption.

and where do we get our knowledge that goes beyond the application of the laws of the natural sciences?

there is no longer an objective reservoir from which we could take it. the eternal verities may have been true until yesterday, today we must derive the criteria of our doings from the doings themselves, from the effects of our making, from the fact of the result.

today we no longer experience humanity as bedded into the forces of nature and belonging to nature; but even the laws of nature have left nature. the laws of nature are the basis of technology, applied in machines and production methods, the manufacture of products and the determination of their use and consumption.

a few generations before us the purpose of nature was seen as being to produce human beings. today nature is degraded to being a mass at the disposal of man and the only problem is how far we can go in exploiting and taking advantage of it without detracting from or destroying the basis of our life, where it is still provided by nature.

the world in which man lived hitherto was the nature that surrounded him, the cosmos in which he stood. and philosophy was the question of how we are connected to this cosmos.

it is only for a little more than a century that philosophy has been concerned with the organizational forms of social life, including the economic conditions of its existence. there is a philosophy of labour, a philosophy of production. there is no philosophy of technology, no philosophy of how technology comes into being, is designed, organized and marketed and subjected to our responsibility. we enjoy practising a philosophy of cognition and of knowledge. a philosophy of making and designing has yet to appear.

man is no longer surrounded by nature and world, but by what he has designed and made. nevertheless making is disparaged. a thinker is looked upon as something better than a maker, someone who organizes is better than someone who produces, the manager is more than the engineer, the university is more than the technical college, a banker is more than a manufacturer. a craftsman is nothing anyway. and someone who grows his own vegetables is laughed at. you can buy them.

the general awareness today that man only becomes a member of society through his actions and activities may go back to marx and hegel. but there are essential differences between activity, working and making. most people only have a job, not work any more. and it is not obvious of someone who works that he makes something. making is an activity for which someone is responsible, in which someone is involved with concept, design, execution and checking. what he makes is under his control and responsibility and is part of himself. making is the extension of the self into the self-organized world. the person is fulfilled in making. and this to the extent that one's own concept, one's own design is involved and perceptions for the correction of concept and design are acquired in constant feedback from making.

only creative making is real work, is development of the person. design is the mark of creativity, and only through it activism and job become humane. a humane world presupposes work and making characterized by design because a person's motive appears in the design.

for hegel all history is the history of an idea, all development that of reason, of global reason, all development the development of a principle. this philosophy, a dangerous philosophy, is firmly anchored in our heads to this day. we abandon ourselves to the way things run, and a person who sees himself as the spirit of the world has the say.

designs make one autonomous, designers are dangerous, dangerous for any sovereign authority. the aggregate condition of our civilization is that of determination. everything is determined, determined by the highest authorities. in consequence our thinking culture too

184

is taught as one of a supreme principle, that of reason. reason as a principle of exclusiveness was raised to the status of a preferred intellectual culture in order to secure the principle of authority.

the principle of purposiveness on the other hand knows no exclusiveness. much is purposive and much is purposive in different ways. the aggregate condition of a purposive world would be plurality. reason clings to the general and universal, the purposive is different from case to case, from subject to subject. in purposiveness the subject reaches agreement with its position, its situation, its case. the purposive needs special initiatives, special designs, it is not general. according to kant, the purposive is orientated towards the particular, not the general.

a culture in the aggregate condition of purposiveness as against a culture of reason would make a thousand initiatives, a thousand concepts, a thousand designs from a supreme idea, a supreme principle. it would take back authority from a supreme principle to the individual. instead of living from definitive causality, instead of living in logical necessity we would live from a "reflective power of judgement" and thus bring about an individual balance between us, environment and world.

in a culture of designs a process comes into being that could be called the decentralization of the truth claim. general reason would return to individual reason, to personal view and power of judgement.

the word reason is often handled in a very contradictory and dubious way. sometimes reason is an organ, sometimes it is a principle. sometimes it is an organ by which we process information in our heads, sometimes it is the principle of conclusiveness and determined causality that even soars up to global reason - be it that of the french revolution or hegel's prussian state.

as an organ of information collection, processing and storage seated in the brain, reason corresponds with our intelligence, as a principle of causality and logical precision it rules the universe, becoming the principle of those who believe they have to rule the world.

in the end people will see that there can be no reason other than the reason in our heads. but by appropriate celebration general reason was raised so high that it exceeds reason in our heads. and this only to rule not only over men, but over heads.

eternal truths, supreme principles, absolute reason, higher insights, general ideas, eternal laws in general do not have rational bases, but social ones. any society based on authority, and this includes the society of industrial civilization, must have, in order to stabilize its substructure, to keep its workers hard at it, a justification in principle. superordinated power is glorified. where the main thing is to paralyse human subjectivity and direct it only towards a general will, whether it be the will of a state, a church or a commercial enterprise, one clings to the world order that there is a supreme reason that drives everything forward. and all the workers get on solidly with their work and collect their pay, all the employees put their ability at the disposal of an employer and draw their salary for that.

as soon as they show signs of developing a need to live according to their own ideas, make their own designs, carry out work according to their own notions, proceed according to their own conceptions, that would be the downfall of those authorities we are all told are necessary for the development and survival of the world.

there are cultural spheres in which creative anarchy is anticipated. given that reason is an organ of information processing and part of the human body, with its seat in the brain, then it must be permissible for eating to count as a human domain with a cultural dimension as well.

today it is impossible not to recognize a trend towards industrial simplification and economic generalization in our nutrition. nevertheless eating and drinking, harvesting and cooking are a cultural sphere that still largely survives without the one great truth. the entire world is concerned with it. chopping, cooking and seasoning are major cultural achievements. we associate great moments in life with eating. it was at banquets that the dialogues came into being through which man recognized himself as a subjective entity. at the centre of the rituals of religion there is something to eat and drink.

this culture has countless traditions and countless initiatives. we involve ourselves in them every day with requests, evaluations and experiments. and yet there are no authorities. there is no truth of cooking. there are as many cuisines as there are ovens. and the grandmother is no less an authority than the gourmet pope from the city of lyons.

but there are dialogues, there are conversations, there are revelations, if you ignore the industries that have their standard recipes laid down by statistics.

how should we feed ourselves? this has become a subject for humanity, also a design subject, a draft subject. and yet there is no central court of appeal that could be said to be in possession of the valid truth. the

186

aggregate condition of this culture is as loose and light as a piece of pastry, yet is still in a position to resist the junk production that has come into being under the banner of maximized profits, and to found a morality of food.

the truth of eating comes from the kitchen. this means that it comes from execution, from doing, from making, from use, just as the individual of the future comes from the decision to live his own life, which first of all means not someone else's life. not that the other life is a heresy. it can be as legitimate as one's own. but the crucial factor of truth is subjectivity, one's own agreement instead of the identifications with general principles. in the whole human culture of eating there are no initiatives other than those of one's own oven.

this is neither intellectual stubbornness nor aristocratic affectation, it is a fundamental requirement. the effect explains the law. the case determines the rule. the use is the truth.

like our food, our behaviour as human beings towards each other and with each other is an open field, an indeterminate relationship. one could arrive at a consensus by pragmatic means. provided that you accepted each person as autonomous and original, like a cuisine. if everyone could trust his design.

the authorities know better. they pronounce ex cathedra. they promulgate decrees. they issue titles and orders to those who support authority. they provide textbooks and make money available for those who can prove the necessity of their existence in every form of pronouncement, in science, also in research, in doctrine and in faith.

there are no professors, no doctors, no recipients of honours in cookery. if there were, it would probably be the end of it. in terms of behaviour outside the kitchen things look different. here truth is not justified, it is rewarded. those people are rewarded who not only support the official truth, the official doctrine or whatever one might call such generalized truths, the general ideology, as beneficiaries, but justify it by pronouncement.

in science, karl popper said, a truth is true until it is replaced by another truth.

in the case of design it is different. every design for which responsibility is assumed is true. what cuisine is more true than another cuisine? what life is more true than another life? what species, to stay with darwin, is more justified than another species? this is not a question of pluralistic tolerance, it is a question of play and its diversity. no science is a pronouncement of truth. science is the pronouncement of a hypothesis. it is a model. and the criterion of a model is not that it is true but that it proves itself.

designers think differently from administrators. the adminstrator speaks for a truth, for an authority, priests for the church, professors for the state university. designers know nothing. all they have to make an approach to something is tools. that makes them suspicious. they need, as jargon has it, a duty book. it is not until they have designed the overall conditions that they apply methods and tools.

the same applies to education. formerly people knew how to bring up children. today we don't know that any more. and that is not because we do not have the appropriate knowledge, but because education is always an individual case. everyone is different. everyone is unique.

the principles literally turn full circle. formerly there were educational principles that had to be applied. now the principles arise as subsequent insights into individual cases. it becomes permissible to arrive at generalizations from the individual act of education. the educator himself is well advised to abandon all general principles and address specific cases. he may certainly take general experience as a guideline, so long as he is prepared to see that his case can contradict all experience. education too is a constructive activity, is the production of development models.

instead of existence, which was the subject of philosophy from parmenides to martin heidegger, we are now faced with the concept of the model. we perceive both what is and also what should be in models of concepts and definitions. access to reality, to the world opens up through a model, a structure of statements, concepts and conceptual operations. and a leap into the future, into a new, possible world, also needs speculation, work on the model. cognition is agreement on the model and future is development of the model. designing means constructing models.

perhaps the mind is more than merely the processing of information. processing is a kind of administrative procedure, linear, one-dimensional. when we speak of mind we mean something different. we mean the ability to form concepts, the ability to develop designs, to "throw something out".

then the concept of mind would be justified as the ability to develop concepts, which means creating multidimensional structures. multidimensional in terms of place, time, method, economy, those involved together with their psychology, and also in terms of aims, purposes, causes, drives.

a design is the most complex structure produced by mental activity. a design is analytical and synthetic at the same time, specific and general, a concrete matter and one of principle. it keeps to the matter in hand and to demands, it goes back to facts and opens up new thinking spaces. it "counts the peas" and opens up perspectives. it calculates and opens up landscapes of possibility.

in designing people come into their own. otherwise they remain civil servants.

people are inclined to see freedom and individuality as a status, as a condition. people think that a human being is free if he lives in conditions of free decision-making. but he does not become free until he realizes freedom, manufactures it. in the most free of societies there can be slaves if people see freedom as habitual behaviour, not as concretization, development, design.

design is the creation of a world. it comes into being at the point at which theory and practice collide. but these do not cancel each other out. they both find ways of developing.

design becomes a new intellectual dimension in its own right alongside theory and practice. human culture can no longer be reduced to thinking and doing. design intervenes as a methodological discipline in its own right, the emergence of something that does not already exist, in either theory or practice. in design both emerge as fundamentals. design transcends theory and practice and not only opens up a new reality, but new insights.

in design, man takes his own development in hand. for human beings, development is no longer nature, but self-development. this is certainly not beyond natural requirements, but does transcend nature. in design man becomes what he is. animals have language and perception as well. but they do not design.

in critical situations it can emerge how little our knowledge and our actions still relate to each other, how much our actions have been disconnected from our insights. we know more than ever about our world and about the threats it faces, threats to nature and climate, threats that come from our civilization, and yet we act and behave in a way that ignores any better knowledge. our intellectualism and rationalism go so far that we even discuss this contradiction in culturally and socially critical terms, display and debate it in terms of public information. but we do not react. we are aware that we are sawing off the branch we are sitting on without limiting our self-destruction. self-alienation is on the increase. we know all too well about the consequences of over-consumption, about the gulf between capital and work, about the balance of resources and waste, about the link between war and profit, but we are no longer capable of getting out of the paralysis that the prosperity of industrial civilization has brought with it. to that extent the person who reminds us that we should take responsibility is no longer credible. responsibility degenerated into a mere response. speaking and doing have become detached from each other. morality is an echo.

this is linked with our educational culture, which is one of knowledge, of reason, down to the belief that our reason could be part of a global reason, participate in the objective spirit that guides and regulates the world.

accordingly, history is the history of a continuing development towards better and higher things, and it is no longer mankind who is murdering and destroying, plundering and exploiting, but the mechanics of the mind.

reason is looking for totality. it will not tolerate anything unreasonable beside it. truth is detached from the concrete and individual to become the general imperative. anyone who is not deluding himself will see a link here between the claims of knowledge and totalitarianism. wrong thinking, here in the tradition of hegel, produces its fateful consequences. we are all the victim of institutions who know better.

the essays in this book are not antirationalist criticism. there are already far too many people involved in the witch-hunt against reason. these essays are based on the experience that there is a reason of acting and making that produces results other than logical derivation with its claim to total truth, and that there is a perception that requires acting and making in the sense that it cannot be acquired without acting and making. it develops by acting and making.

a cathedral is not the application of static knowledge, is not academic cleverness, it is the product of a culture of making, of designing, of reason in action. technology is not mastered by the person who knows about it and therefore prescribes structural conditions for it in the awareness of moral responsibility. technology is mastered by the person who can handle and control it as technology. there are other sources of cognition than understanding and reason. even kant tracked down a third cognition alongside understanding and reason, which he called *urteilskraft*, the power of judgement. this aimed not at the general, but at the concrete in its circumstances, which is the same thing as changing it.

this book is concerned with the dimension of design itself. here design is not seen as refinement, beautification, presentation. the notion of drafting is to be found in the original meaning of the word. design is first of all drafting, blueprint, even though the word has come predominantly to mean aesthetic cosmetics in the mean time. a design culture can be seen as a culture of coming to terms with this world, rather than taking refuge in compensatory aesthetics. then design moves into the proximity of active reason.

many of the essays are polemical in their prevailing tone. this is not literary in motivation, it is not style, but derives from excitement. the world is becoming more beautiful and pleasant to the extent that we are destroying it. this also has an effect on language, especially at points where it deals with given causes. some of the essays refer to subjects from an institution called "institute of analoguous studies", and these studies are derived from a way of thinking that is aimed not at knowledge, but at judgement, meaning that it includes decision. a judgement of this kind refers to states of affairs and situations. thinking of this kind is not content with generalizable insights. it is concerned with cases and situations. its judgements are statements on a topic, taking up a position. in such cases thinking in pictures, imagination, an analoguous approach is particularly important. work at the institute moves in the context of visual thinking and visual language and lives from the experience of creative activity.

sources

"krise der moderne", lecture to the architectural faculty of the university of karslruhe for the 60th anniversary of the foundation of the dammerstock estate, 1989.

"die dritte moderne", *arch+*, no. 102 (january 1990).

"hans gugelot", in *hans gugelot. systemdesign*, exhibition catalogue, munich 1983.

"flugapparate von paul mc cready" in lufthansa's annual report for 1981.

"bauhaus und ulm", in herbert lindinger (ed.), *hochschule für gestaltung ulm. die moral der gegenstände*, berlin 1987.

"architektur als abbild des staates", lecture to the architectural faculty of the university of stuttgart, 1983.

"der nicht mehr brauchbare gebrauchsgegenstand", in *türklinken. Workshop in brakel*, cologne 1987.

"die unterschrift", in *johannes potente, brakel. design der 50erjahre*, cologne 1989.

"schwierigkeiten für architekten und designer", in *die küche zum kochen*, munich 1982.

"erscheinungsbild", in *ERCO lichtfabrik*, berlin 1990.

"der freiraum des grafikers", in *in rotis*, no place, 1987.

"eine neue schrift", in *in rotis*, no place, 1987.

Printed in the USA
CPSIA information can be obtained
at www.ICGtesting.com
LVHW050928211223
766828LV00013B/167